MURDER
IN THE
CHURCH

Other books by Chris Schimel...

Touch One - Creation House;

Beautiful Behaviors - Creation House

Once Broken - Evergreen Press

I Do, Do You? - Author Academy Elite

E-Books

Lessons of the Fall

Between You and Me

A Story of Rage

Ripples

See the back pages of this book for book descriptions.

MURDER IN THE CHURCH

When Spiritual Weakness and Abusive Power Collide

Chris Schimel

Paperback ISBN : 978-1-64746-080-8

Hardback ISBN: 978-1-64746-081-5

Ebook ISBN: 978-1-64746-082-2

Library of Congress Control Number: 2019920549

This story is based on true accounts that occurred in a church the
author led as pastor. Names, times and locations have been changed to
protect privacies.

Dedication

Were it not for these people, many things in my life and the lives of those in my family, including the publishing of this book, would not have been possible. I gratefully dedicate this book to them.

Jerry and Korena Rothlisberger
&
Chuck and Terry Parks
&
John and Marilyn Hemmer
&
Michael Hemmer

TABLE OF CONTENTS

FOREWORD

I knew Chris Schimel and his wife Shirley when I initially became a Christian in the first church I attended in Southern California. Shirley and I sang and played together in the first band I took part in as a believer. In that church I recall singing in front of Keith Green, after which Chris offered a short sermon to conclude the concert. They were good days in my brand-new walk with the Lord.

There was more than one time that I would go over to Chris' house with my guitar to run some of my first songs by them to gain feedback. When Chris left that church to take his first pastorate, he invited me to come and present my first concert away from my home church, at his church in South Gate, California. I remember singing "The King is Coming."

I knew Chris to be a dedicated and caring pastor back then. But in his book *Murder in the Church* it is clear he takes dedication and caring to a whole new level, not by his choice, but by God's. I don't think I have ever seen a pastor drawn into a parishioner's crisis in the way Pastor Chris is drawn into the one contained in this book. The story is marked with tragedy, and yet, the way God redeems is truly remarkable. It is one of the most unbelievable accounts I have ever been exposed to. This story will take your breath away—several times; and finally, do so with a flash of God's Glory.

Furthermore, this story, along with the lessons it teaches, addresses issues of our day that are timely and enlightening concerning the sovereignty, grace and mercy of God. My appraisal is that this story is less about the people involved, and more about the eternal purposes of God and his Son Jesus Christ.

I invite you into this adventure called *Murder in the Church*. But, be prepared; because it just may change you.

Carman – Gospel Music Icon

PREFACE

This is more than a heart-pounding story. It is a minute-by-minute account of a true murderous event set in a church with the author as its pastor.

The story stands alone as an account anyone could learn from. As you read you will observe teachable moments jumping out at you from the pages. However, the author makes a point to identify eye-opening, life-changing lessons to conclude the book that will bring unmistakable substance and soul-search-ability to the remarkable story you are about to read.

In this story you will find references that suggest that this event wasn't just foretold and watched over by the Lord; you'll learn why it is a story that would affect the entirety of the author's life and ministry. He would not just write it and rewrite it for publication; he would find himself reliving the power and the truth of the story in all aspects of his life and ministry, writing other books that address the life lessons in the story and watching people he leads wrestle with those same lessons repeatedly. Furthermore, he is moved to emotion every few weeks as some aspect of the story comes to mind.

This isn't just a story that is here today and gone tomorrow. It is a story that has timeless implications. It happened in a segment of time; but its lessons will be relevant to people's lives for many generations regardless of what new technology or generational personalities may present; or whatever new people personality groups may emerge.

It isn't a story that happened. It is a story that happens. The circumstances may be different, and the consequences may vary, but the story happens every day. It is, no doubt, why the author believes that God wanted it to be told.

Murder in the Church was written to help people. You will see clearly that severe consequences can happen to those who make bad choices—choices some may be in the process of making even now. However, amid the dark and difficult consequences, as His word continues to illustrate, God is prepared to allow His light to shine through with redemptive brilliance.

Day One
A SATURDAY ONE SEPTEMBER

I t began on a Saturday night. Our phone rang at about 10:15.

As pastors, anytime we receive a call after nine thirty or so, we hold our breath. But Saturday nights are the worst because of the importance of the day that follows. A late Saturday night call usually meant an empty post in some area of ministry the next day, one we would have to fill.

I was in our downstairs storage area getting ready for a camping trip I was going to be making in a few weeks, when I heard the phone rattle off its familiar series of rings. Because it was so late and realizing it to be a Saturday night call, my apprehension rose quickly, and I stopped what I was doing to listen. But all I could hear through the walls was mumbling, so I went on with what I was doing.

"Hi, Sarah," my wife Shirley told me later the conversation began. Then she asked, "Sarah, is everything all right?"

Speaking in a calm and controlled voice, Sarah said, "Well, that's why I'm calling. I thought I should tell you that Raymond just left me for another man."

Shirley's first reaction wasn't shock. It was disbelief. Sarah's proper, carefully spoken words, along with the unusual message she placed before my wife, caused her to think, just for a moment, that Sarah was kidding. But Shirley caught herself before she laughed, and responded, "Excuse me, Sarah. What did you just say?"

Sarah repeated herself, continuing to talk in an unusually controlled and formal voice for normal conversation, let alone for communicating the bombshell of a lifetime.

Still downstairs, I continued compiling my gear but kept one ear aimed upstairs to see if the mumbling would stop.

"I know it sounds a bit unusual, but you remember Daniel Rogers, don't you? He visited our church a few weeks ago. Well, I told you about our dinner party tonight. Raymond insisted that Daniel attend. So, I agreed. We all had a wonderful time. Daniel seemed to have a bit of a smirk on his face for most of the evening, but I didn't think much about it because I was having such a good time laughing and visiting with our friends."

Sarah went on, "After our guests left, Raymond asked if he and Daniel could talk to me for a few minutes. I agreed, and we sat down at the kitchen table. That is where he told me that he and Daniel were lovers, that he has had affairs with other men, and he has discovered he is gay. He and Daniel want to go into business together, be lovers, and he wants me to start divorce proceedings this week. He left tonight to move in with Daniel."

My wife took a long, deep breath, and then, after a longer pause, asked sympathetically, "Sarah, do you want Chris and I to come over to be with you and pray with you?"

That is when curiosity got the best of me. I came up the stairs and walked into the room just in time to see the puzzled look on my wife's face. I could tell all was not fine.

Shirley's mouth was open in awe. As I came to a stop and stood in front of her, her eyes told the story. As if she knew exactly why I had come upstairs, they shouted, "This call does not represent your typical emergency. It represents more—much more!"

Her eyes looking into mine, communicated a mixture of dismay, disbelief, and horror all at the same time. But I was clueless. I stood in front of her and listened with great anticipation in order to grasp some understanding of what was going on.

In response to Shirley's question, Sarah said, "No, you don't need to come over. Christina will be coming home from work soon, and I will need to talk with her. I think it is best that I talk to her by herself first. I guess I owe that to her as our daughter. I don't think I'll come to church in the morning if that's all right. I want to stay near the phone in case Raymond calls."

"I understand. Listen Sarah, we are busy all day tomorrow with a lunch and a leadership meeting, and we won't be done until about eight-thirty. We can come over then, or we can cancel our lunch after church."

"No, don't cancel anything. Raymond will probably come over tomorrow and if you are here, he might not come in if he feels ashamed in front of you. If eight-thirty is all right for you, it's fine for me too."

Then turning and looking away to regain her focus, Shirley said, "Sarah, let me pray with you."

She prayed a prayer that showed concern for Sarah and Raymond, but not with words that would clue me into the problem. Then she hung up the phone and stared straight ahead not saying a word. I waited as long as I could, attempting to allow her time to tell me the scoop on her own—perhaps five seconds.

I finally prodded, "Well, what is it?"

She answered, "Raymond . . . left Sarah . . . are you ready for this . . . for another man!"

I had to sit down.

LOOKING BACK

Little did we know that call would be the beginning of a nine-day long journey for us to hell and back.

But hell began much earlier for Raymond.

Raymond's home during his early years was dominated by positive female influences and negative male influences. Raymond was a helpless and unaware victim of the dysfunctional forces associated with these early imprints upon his psyche.

During Raymond's impressionable years, he heard so much yelling and screaming from his father that his home seemed more like a battlefield than a family. When the kids did something wrong such as break a vase or smudge the carpet, his mom would come to their rescue. She would hide the indiscretion and repair the broken or disfigured item before their father could find out about it.

She wasn't an enabler; she was a savior. If she didn't take on that role, their father would fly into one of his angry tirades and terrorize her vulnerable children or her. Raymond felt it was "us against him."

When Raymond's father did witness or find out about a miscue, he would find something to hit with as quickly as he could—a strap, a belt, or something more solid. Then he would come out swinging.

While growing up, as with most kids, Raymond and his sisters were involved in activities in the school they attended, such as plays, concerts, sports, and the like. His dad never came to watch—not even once. His mother was there, but his father would never darken the school doors. It seemed he felt that his job was to work and watch television. He felt that supporting his kids in their activities, their involvements, and their lives, was simply not in his job description.

Raymond's father also had a favorite word. *Stupid!* He used it freely to describe the things he disapproved of. It wouldn't have been so bad if the members of his family weren't the primary objects of his disapproval. Some of the standout memories Raymond had of his father were the times when he would berate his son with this destructive word. "Raymond, how could you do such a *stupid* thing?" "Your idea is *stupid*." "Everything you do is *stupid*." "Everything you say is *stupid*." "Raymond, *you* are *stupid*."

This would explain why Raymond never felt like his father approved of anything he was, did, or said. Raymond's recollection was that he never heard his father voice approving words in his direction—ever. From the time Raymond was born until his father died at eighty, this held true. Never did he hear, "Good job, son," or "Good idea, Raymond." Never did he hear, "Good try," or, "You're a good kid." A more accurate remembrance of his father's words was, "Raymond, you are good for nothing."

Furthermore, Raymond never received a hug, a smile, a wink, or a pat on the back suggesting that his father felt well or proud of him.

In Raymond's memory, his father never gave him anything, bought him anything, encouraged him in anything, or complimented him for anything. He only made Raymond feel bad.

Other issues were present as well. At a certain point in his young life, Raymond decided competitive sports were not his cup of tea. This, perhaps, was the issue that once and for all, broke down what little camaraderie may have potentially existed between Raymond and his father.

You see Raymond's dad was a sports fanatic. He watched every game on television, listened by radio to the games not televised, and read the sport's section of the newspaper at the same time. He thought sports were all there was to life. He didn't have time for a son who thought differently.

In contrast, Raymond's mother was exemplary. She attended every function her kids participated in at school. She tucked the kids in at night, gave them affection, and told them she loved them. When funds permitted, she bought toys, candy, ice cream cones, and other treats for them. She did so from her own earnings, because Raymond's father refused to part with his money for such frivolous kindnesses for his children.

Compared to how he felt about his father, Raymond's mother was his hero and heroine. His sisters and mom were his friends, fellow soldiers and comrades in arms, in battle against the evil and masculine tyrant who oppressed his formative years.

In later years, when asked if he hated his father, he would respond, "No, I just feel sorry for him." This translated to an overwhelming lack of respect that Raymond held for his dad.

What Raymond didn't realize was that, somewhere down deep in the inner recesses of his soul, another kind of disrespect was also brewing—disrespect for maleness and a lack of trust for the whole concept of manhood. Along with that, confusion was developing in his heart about what a man should be. The only example he had of a man was the poor example of his father.

No one could say for sure that these feelings translated into a full-blown rejection of heterosexuality. But at the very least, it raised the level of curiosity for gayness in his soul.

One can only imagine from these early abuses, that Raymond struggled with self-esteem issues his whole life. He questioned his identity, his abilities, his self-image, and, at a certain point, his sexual identity.

His soul had been bruised. This was the beginning of the "hell" in Raymond's life. But this whole era in Raymond's adolescent years wasn't the only factor influencing him to consider other options sexually.

By the summer prior to the fateful September, Raymond had been married to Sarah for almost thirty years. Their early marriage seemed to be vibrant enough, but over time it grew cold.

Their daughter, Christina, became their focus. Raymond loved his daughter, but his flame for Sarah was flickering badly. By the time of the woeful Saturday night phone call Raymond had not been intimate with his wife for ten years.

Raymond constantly picked on Sarah for her foolishness and her lack of attentiveness to the details of the house, such as cleaning, cooking, and so forth.

While Raymond picked, Sarah would nag at him for his forgetfulness, his lack of discipline in monetary issues, and in her estimation, his dull-wittedness. In short, virtually no expressions of love, affection, or intimacy were being exchanged between them, and attraction for each other was by this time nonexistent. They weren't husband and wife; they were room-mates; and they were maintaining a casual relationship at best.

Alone, these two very real problems were plenty to bait the trap of gay curiosity in Raymond's heart, but there was more.

TRYING GOD

About the time Raymond met and married Sarah, he also met some people who were Christians. These people became close lifetime friends. They brought Raymond and Sarah to church, and after a few services, when an invitation was given for people to become Christians, Raymond and Sarah both responded. Sarah felt and experienced very real emotions and changes in her life, but not so Raymond. He was moved by the message and the service, and really wanted to invite Christ into his life—which he did. But that is where it seemed to stop. He never felt moved again. He never felt the fresh, new vibrancy of the Christian "born-again" experience. Something prevented Raymond from experiencing God, growing in Him, or even knowing Him.

The human relationships Raymond developed were good, but they weren't the kind that fostered an environment of accountability. None of his friends felt the freedom to chal-lenge Raymond concerning his coldness toward Christ, maybe because that kind of accountability in relationships wasn't taught back then. Or perhaps it was because those friends never got close enough to Raymond to detect it; or it could be that Raymond himself wouldn't allow it.

Whatever the cause, these friendships forfeited further intimacy when an ugly church split occurred. Contact waned and any hope of healthy confrontation for Raymond was whisked away in the throes of relational separations.

So, Raymond was left pretty much on his own. Concerning his spiritual choices, he shot from the hip. Carnal persuasions were largely what he relied on to make his choices in most every area of his life; family, work, relationships and church. With Raymond, it was as it was in the Old Testament passage: [He] *"did what was right in his own eyes"* (Judges 17:6). As a result of this, people seemed to back away from him.

All of this computed to an alienation Raymond created in his own heart toward the only relationships in his life that could rescue him. He had sabotaged the last and final connection he had with people who could confront him about the lifestyle he was already becoming enslaved to.

EXPERIMENTATION

Raymond worked for many years at a large aeronautical corporation. At a certain point, he had the idea of starting his own construction business along the lines of some work experience he had received earlier in his life. It would allow Raymond to be his own boss, and there seemed to be a great need for construction workers with all the new housing going up in our area. After much thought, he went for it.

It wasn't a lucrative endeavor. Apparently, there was more competition in Raymond's area of construction than he had anticipated. But he plunged in just the same. It brought in enough to pay the bills for Raymond and Sarah, but not a lot more and it went on this way for many years.

Often the workload demanded for Raymond to hire extra help to get the jobs done in a timely manner. But since finances were tight, he would hire day laborers and pay them a nominal wage under the table. Over the years Raymond discovered he had a soft spot in his heart for these "down-on-their-luck" unfortunates.

However, another factor surfaced in all of this. Nearing sixty years of age, Raymond found he no longer had the physical strength or stamina to do the hard work his job required all by himself. So, he began to rely on the youth and vitality of the "down and outers" he found in the different labor pools he frequented.

None of us knew Raymond had already begun to experiment with gay relationships. Sometime before the fateful Saturday night call, Raymond began visiting a pornographic bookstore down the street from one of his construction material suppliers. He started looking into smut of the heterosexual variety, but at a certain point that changed.

Then, for several months, he experimented with this new and different pleasure. Soon he was going to more than one of these bookstores, and during this time he had a few sexual encounters with other men. They didn't constitute sexual intercourse, but they paved the way, each encounter eliminating certain barriers that were acting as roadblocks to gayness for Raymond.

Then, in July, two months before Day One, Raymond met someone at one of the bookstores.

One sinister, hot summer day, when Raymond was at one of his wood suppliers checking out material costs for a future construction job, he stopped by one of the bookstores in the vicinity of the lumberyard.

It was then and there he met Daniel Rogers. That day, Raymond crossed over from experimentation into a full-blown gay relationship with this complete stranger. No doubt, Raymond's guard had been let down from the many tough luck cases he had hired with no backlash.

And Daniel seemed like such a nice guy.

He wasn't a large man. He stood only five feet ten inches tall. Nor was he heavy, only weighing about one hundred and eighty pounds. But he owned a solid frame—healthy, toned, and muscular. He had dirty blonde hair, but it was shaved to perhaps a quarter inch in length all over his head, with a slight receding hairline.

Daniel's face revealed a hard life. Though he was in his early to mid-forties, he looked perhaps ten years older than he was. He seldom smiled, which caused people to feel it could constitute danger to stare at him for more than a few seconds. His eyes always seemed to be wide open and round, but you could feel him squinting at you in mistrust just the same. In a crowd he didn't portray himself as one wanting to be noticed. Instead, he seemed to slide from corner to corner and place himself near doors he could slip out of if he needed to, as if he were afraid of people; or worse yet, had things to hide.

Prior to meeting Raymond, Daniel Rogers had not worked in the type of construction business Raymond was in. But he was a hard worker and a perfect profile of the down-on-their-luck kind of individuals Raymond was used to digging up. But this was different—very different.

First, there was the gay relationship between Raymond and Daniel. This profoundly complicated the situation. Raymond found himself a bit lovesick. For the first time in years he was having fun with love, although a severe kind of guilt was tainting all his feelings. He was neck-deep in a type of love he knew nothing about.

At the same time, Daniel was a surprise relief for Raymond. He was strong and healthy physically. As a result, he was able to do a lot of the hard work that was becoming especially difficult for Raymond. In addition, because Daniel was Raymond's lover, Daniel took on the role of protector. He made Raymond feel, if he allowed Daniel to be involved with him and his business, he would make sure Raymond never had to risk hurting himself with heavy work again. All of this was very appealing to Raymond and played into his imminent decisions concerning his relationship with Daniel.

Next, there was the severity of Daniel's hard-luck circumstances. He wasn't just a man down on his luck. He had been in prison and was released only a few short weeks before meeting Raymond. He had spent the last several years in a state institution for some very serious crimes, and his prison sentence had dissolved all his connections. Daniel Rogers was friendless, moneyless, jobless, and almost hopeless regarding future options.

To add to the difficulty of his plight, he was saddled with extremely oppressive parole requirements. Furthermore, he had no transportation and no assistance amid a profoundly desperate place in his life. He needed more than help. He needed a savior...much like Raymond.

These were all tough concerns, however, the issue of Daniel Rogers' life that made his connection with Raymond more different than any other Raymond had ever encountered was the control.

Daniel was sick. Yes, he was streetwise. And yes, he was gay. He was also desperate. Above all else, however, he was an out-of-control controller, and would allow no person to control him.

Daniel was a master of manipulation and oppressive power. Raymond didn't see it at first, but as their relationship stretched into weeks, and as they became more entangled emotionally and sexually, Raymond found he had met his match. For as intimidating and controlling as Raymond had become over the years, probably the result of anger from the early abuses in his life; Daniel Rogers was stronger. He was more cunning, more subtle, more overpowering psychologically, and more manipulative than Raymond could ever be even when he was at his worst.

In less than two months Daniel Rogers had convinced Raymond to leave his wife and beloved daughter, move into an apartment with him, fully furnish that apartment, pay for the rent and move in costs, begin divorce proceedings with Sarah, make him half owner in Raymond's construction business, and turn Raymond's business cell phone over to him.

Sarah had no idea concerning the power Daniel was wielding over her husband; and, Raymond was also clueless as to the darkness that lurked inside the heart of Daniel Rogers.

DINNER PARTY

A week prior to Day One, Raymond and Sarah decided to have a few couples over to their house for dinner. They scheduled it for seven o'clock on Saturday evening about three hours prior to Sarah's call to my wife. On the morning of the dinner, Raymond announced to Sarah that he would like Daniel to come to the dinner party that night as well. Sarah was not at all in favor of this. She had begun to feel uneasy about Daniel and all the time Raymond was spending with him. By this time, Raymond had leaked the truth about Daniel's criminal past to Sarah in a verbal miscue. After the lip-slip Raymond swore her to secrecy. It all heightened Sarah's concern about Daniel; but every time she even lightly broached the subject, Raymond would embarrass her for judging Daniel and make her feel ashamed for bringing up her fears in the first place.

Sarah had also begun to entertain suspicions about Raymond's and Daniel's relationship. *Could I be jealous of Daniel's and Raymond's friendship and the time they spend together?* She thought. *Nonsense!* And she would quickly tell herself . . . *that's silly.*

At other times, even if it were just for a moment, she would wonder . . . *could Raymond and Daniel be lovers? That's impossible! Not Raymond!* She would even smile at how ludicrous that prospect sounded and just as quickly dismiss the idea.

When Raymond informed Sarah that Daniel would attend the party, Daniel was standing on the front porch outside their house.

"Why does he have to come?" Sarah barked at Raymond.

"Do you have a problem with Daniel?" Raymond retorted quite a bit louder than Sarah had spoken and loud enough for Daniel to hear through the screen door.

They argued about it for a few minutes and finally Raymond put his foot down and said, "Well, he's coming whether you like it or not," and walked out the door.

There were also other things Sarah had begun to notice that didn't seem right but was unable to put all the pieces together.

First, it seemed Raymond and Daniel were never apart; not just during the day when daylight permitted construction work, but in the evening as well. Occasionally, they would be at the Gil's house, but usually they were elsewhere.

When Sarah would ask where he had been, Raymond would typically answer, "Daniel and I were doing some business planning."

Sarah thought this peculiar since Raymond had never had these kinds of planning meetings before with any of his laborers in all the ten years he had been working in his construction business. Besides, never before had Raymond gotten this close to any of the workers he had hired.

In fact, at different times Raymond would say, "It is probably good that I don't get too close to the guys I hire from the labor pools, because I don't know anything about them." Wisdom demanded it. Now, here he was, violating his own safety code with Daniel. Sarah thought this strange as well.

All these things concerned Sarah about Daniel, but she conceded to her husband's request about the dinner party with many inner reservations. She was beginning to resent what she perceived to be an unwelcome addition to the Gil family lifestyle, and she felt it strongly that day. She had not yet said it aloud to Raymond but resolved that she *would* very soon.

That evening, the guests were to arrive around seven. Raymond showed up with Daniel at quarter of, and they were waiting in the living room as company came to the door.

Raymond welcomed the guests and introduced them to his friend. Sarah tried to appear busy in the kitchen because she didn't want to sit and converse with Daniel.

Dinner went fine. There was laughter, stories, and gracious compliments about the food. Daniel and Raymond seemed a little quiet, but for the most part Sarah forgot her discomfort with Daniel.

A little before eight, however, Raymond announced he needed to take Daniel home for something. This raised Sarah's stress level and weighed down her mind considerably until they returned. They were gone for about half an hour.

When they returned, the atmosphere of the dinner party changed dramatically. Both Raymond and Daniel were quiet and stone-faced, almost as if they had been in a fight. Sarah even searched for redness or bruises on Raymond's face, thinking they might have struck each other, but saw none.

The night wound down quickly after that, as did the comfort of their guests. They said their good-byes and by nine-thirty, Raymond, Sarah, and Daniel were left alone in the Gil home. Sarah went immediately into the kitchen to clean up and the two men followed.

Raymond said nervously, "Uh…Sarah, before you get into that, could you sit down? We have something we need to talk to you about."

There was a small, rectangular table against a wall with three chairs around it in the kitchen that served as a breakfast and quick-meal site for the three Gils. It was a perfect setting for Raymond's announcement.

Raymond began, "Sarah, we have something to tell you."

Sarah has always loved to entertain. Over the years she and Raymond would have people over for dinners, parties, and get-togethers; and after the gatherings were over, she would be on a kind of "high" from the good time she had experienced. This night was somewhat that way as well.

Despite Raymond and Daniel's half-hour absence, the dinner had been filled with fun and fellowship and caused Sarah to forget most of her personal issues with Daniel. As she sat down with the two of them, her alarm was not sounding. Instead she was still enjoying a sense of merriment in her heart from the evening. This made Raymond's announcement even more of a mind blower.

Raymond went on, "Daniel and I have been doing a lot of talking and planning concerning the business, and . . . uh . . . we . . . I . . . have decided to make Daniel a half owner in my business."

The merriment in Sarah's heart came to a sudden, shocking halt.

Raymond's business, though it had done so meagerly, had supplied their livelihood for a decade. What would a partner do to their family's economics? Besides, if there were ever to be a partner in Raymond's business, she thought it should be her. In her mind she was trying to decipher the message and compute the mathematics of what that would mean. But she didn't have time, because the next jarring pronouncement came right on its heels. Raymond didn't give her time to catch her breath.

Glancing quickly in Daniel's direction and then back to Sarah, Raymond said, "Since I met Daniel, I have discovered that I am not heterosexual."

When Sarah tilted her head and looked at Raymond perplexed, he said bluntly, "I'm homosexual, Sarah. I've been experimenting with this lifestyle for some time now, and I have had more than one encounter with other men over the past few years. I am gay, Sarah."

But the bewildered look on Sarah's face didn't reflect her confusion with the terms. It reflected the confusion in her mind with how it could be.

Raymond looked quickly over at Daniel again but didn't look back at Sarah. Instead, he looked down and to the side as he said, "Dan and I have become lovers, and I am moving out of the house tonight and into an apartment with him."

Sarah's mouth flew open, and she felt her eyes become as round as saucers. Inside her head she could feel all the wheels moving and grinding, shearing off gears, and trying to send messages to her mouth to speak, but couldn't form any words.

She only had enough presence of mind to glance over at Daniel. He wasn't looking at her though, or around the room in shame. Instead, he was looking at Raymond, and with his eyes, seemed to be giving him encouragement and approval.

She looked back at Raymond, still with no words to speak. Sarah sensed a scream churning deep within her and probably would have released it if she had been given the opportunity to allow it to develop. But Raymond didn't afford her that opportunity. Rather, he hit Sarah with a third staggering proclamation.

He said, "Sarah, I know this is all a shock, but there's one more thing that is going to be necessary because of all this. You need to file for divorce, and it needs to be in the next week."

Sarah really didn't know what to say. Anger, retaliation, or disgust weren't what rushed to her mind, and the scream never materialized. Instead, she said calmly, "Well, Raymond, if that is what you feel you need to do, then, I guess that is the way it will have to be. You had better get some things together so you can leave."

Raymond, feeling a bit bewildered himself that Sarah didn't shout and throw things, moved quickly. He pushed his chair back from the table and hurried down the hall to their bedroom to grab some needed items. Daniel stood up and placed himself in the entryway between the kitchen where Sarah was sitting, and the hall leading to the bedrooms. He appeared to be acting as a barrier between the two spouses he had just split up.

It seemed to Sarah that Raymond must have grabbed up only the most necessary items that he could gather in a few minutes because he was coming back down the hall in a very short time. When Daniel saw him coming, he slipped out the front door. Sarah just remained at the kitchen table, staring straight ahead—unable to speak—unable to move.

As Raymond turned toward the front door, he paused to look at Sarah. As their eyes met, Raymond said, "I'll get the rest of my things tomorrow." Then, with an expression that looked to Sarah like guilt and remorse, he stepped into the kitchen to where Sarah was seated, leaned over, and kissed her lightly on the cheek.

"I'll talk to you tomorrow," he said. With that, he returned to the entryway and walked out the door.

Sarah stood and stepped over to the kitchen window. There was enough light coming from the house for her to see Raymond walk quickly toward his van. He disappeared from sight, however, as he left the weak beam of light being projected from the window and stepped into the darkness. She heard two car-doors slam and the engine start. The headlights came on and Raymond's van backed out of the driveway.

Sarah sat back down at the kitchen table and again, stared straight ahead. One lone tear came to one eye, but that was all. It was as if her confused emotions at the time were begging to be expressed, but some unknown force inside her took immediate control and abruptly prohibited their release. The one tear stayed in her eye and just dried up.

As she sat there, she thought . . . *After so many spats, angry words, cold stares, and verbal jabs; of all the times that I imagined his leaving or my leaving, I never thought I would feel like this. This is what it must be like to feel numb.*

But Sarah wasn't numb. She was in shock—genuine, panic-stricken, traumatic shock.

She waited a few minutes to collect her thoughts, and then reasoned, "I'd better call Pastor Chris and Shirley." She dialed our number as she glanced at the clock. It was quarter after ten.

Shirley and I were unable to find words to contribute to a discussion about the news we had just heard. We stared at each other, shaking our heads in bewilderment for several moments, not that the news about Raymond was possible but that we had never seen it coming. I think Sarah's phone call left us in our own kind of shock.

We were too amazed and confused to talk much about what we had just heard, and it was a Saturday night. We needed to get some sleep before the next day. But we also felt, considering the seriousness of the situation, it was inappropriate to talk about anything else. We were able to muster enough presence of mind to pray together for the Gil family, but no other conversation seemed proper. So, we went off to bed.

That was Day One

DAY TWO
SUNDAY

Raymond wasn't the most loveable church member I have had over the years. Nor was he the least. He actually had a very tender side. He always seemed to be on the lookout for the underdog and the less fortunate in order to help them in some way. He also had a giving heart. Even though his own financial condition wasn't the best, he often found someone in need—someone to whom he could offer money or assistance. In addition, he was a servant. He enjoyed helping people and doing tasks for the church and those in leadership. These are exceptional qualities.

Raymond's most troublesome issues had to do with the level of negative feelings he had about himself. All of us struggle with this to a degree, some more than others, and various reasons are to blame. But Raymond's personal identity problems came largely from his very soiled upbringing—more soiled than many—and it created a lot of baggage that seemed to get him into most of his messes.

First, Raymond had a lot of opinions and suggestions about the way he thought things should be. His life was centered in the church, so that is where he expressed most of his grievances. When leadership didn't agree, typically, he would take offense and jump on a bandwagon about his opinion, talking to others to rally support for his idea. He probably did this just so he would feel better about himself, because in talking to others, eventually, he could find agreement with his point of view.

The problems with this are obvious. Besides the church disunity that can result, when someone has a lot of suggestions mingled with confidence deficiencies, their suggestions often transform into criticisms, and from there, into divisive fault-finding. I don't think Raymond had evil intent with his disagreements. I think it was merely a natural result of the early trauma in his life, and his resulting poor self-image.

In addition, Raymond had the capacity to get easily upset at people who challenged him, such as customers who didn't like his work or refused to pay on time. He had a restraining order placed on him for what one customer felt was harassment from him. He had a way of exaggerating issues and then taking those issues to the extreme and he did the same with issues in the church.

In addition to some of the things we have already said about Raymond, he was not at all discreet in his communication to his family about his frustrations outside the church and in. Nor was he careful to shelter his family from the things he felt critical of in the church.

His wife received an earful every time her husband didn't like something, which was often. From time to time she tried to defend the church and its leadership, but a constant barrage of critical fire is hard to ward off indefinitely. So, with each negative assessment, eventually, Raymond won Sarah over, if just in trust.

Nor was Raymond guarded about his criticisms in front of his daughter. Most every gripe he had found its way to Christina's ears.

I recall about a year and a half before Day One, our youth minister wanted to have a "Question-and-Answer Night with the Pastor." The youth could ask me any question they wanted.

They wrote their questions out the week before, and I had seven days to analyze and ponder answers for them.

All their questions were theological or organizational in nature...except Christina's. Hers were critical and parroted all the criticisms her father had posed to me at different times. I tried to answer them objectively and with non-threatened feelings. But I felt great despair for Christina. She was a helpless victim and seemed doomed to have the same negative attitude her father possessed. She was being given both a model and permission to follow in her father's footsteps.

Though I tried not to be paranoid, it seemed from that point on I received a cold shoulder from Christina. She was jovial with others, but not with me. When I would try to engage her in even light conversation, she would find an excuse to end the communication and get away. I remember thinking that there could be only one explanation. Raymond had been as loose with his criticisms in front of Christina as he had been with others. What broke my heart the most was that I knew Christina's relationship with God wasn't as strong as it could be; and I knew her attitude toward me would diminish her ability to receive instruction from me as her pastor.

One would expect that I would have no desire to help this man and his family who had been the source of grief for me. In fact, some may think I should have been gloating in their misfortune and feeling they were just getting what they deserved. But I wasn't.

However, to say that I was quick to spring to their aid would not be accurate either.

I didn't hate Raymond. I couldn't. Jesus wouldn't allow me that liberty. But the Sunday morning following Sarah's call to us, I was definitely having trouble summoning deep concern regarding the matter. I don't think it was that I preferred Raymond leave our church, although the current scenario seemed to be providing that ultimate outcome. Nor do I think I was feeling that his critical spirit was "reaping what it had sown" its whole life. No, I didn't feel either of those things. But on that Sunday morning, the urgency factor in my heart for the Gil family's present plight was clearly in a diminished state.

My routine on Sunday mornings since becoming a pastor has been to wake up early in the morning and study my already-prepared sermon for two additional hours. I have stuck to this routine for all my years as a pastor.

Upon rising that morning, I didn't even recall the previous night's phone call until Shirley brought it to my remembrance. At seven thirty she walked into the room where I was studying, and asked, "What are you going to say about what is going on with the Gils this morning?"

I didn't tell her I had forgotten. I said, "You know, I . . . I . . . I wasn't sure where I was going to put it. My thinking was maybe . . . uh . . . during the prayer time. You know, I'll just pray this morning and I'll mention it in my prayer anonymously, so as not to raise questions and embarrass them."

She seemed satisfied with my response, but for just a moment I paused to question my own motives. *Why had I forgotten?* I wondered . . . *was it my subconscious way of passively, but aggressively, taking out my vengeance on Raymond for all the fiery darts he had thrown at me over the years?* I am not sure I fully dismissed the idea, but I shook off my meditations about it all, as I still had more studying to do before we would leave for church.

During the morning service I prayed for the Gil situation as I had told my wife I would—carefully, professionally, and anonymously. No one said anything to me about them that morning, making me aware that Shirley and I were the only ones who knew. Sarah, (as she had said the night before), Christina, and of course Raymond, didn't attend service that morning, so there were no information sources at church to divulge what was happening with the family. No one ever asks about the details of the "unspoken request," so we were the only ones aware of the situation.

After church, Shirley and I went to lunch to fulfill our Sunday afternoon dinner obligations and our time was quite enjoyable. We had lunch with old friends who were visiting in the area, and we laughed ourselves silly.

Parking Lot Meeting

Ironically, while we laughed about old times, on the other side of town, things weren't nearly as jovial.

When Christina came home Saturday night, Sarah sat her down and gave her the news—the awful news. Her reaction wasn't shock, or surprise. It was utter disbelief and denial.

She said to her mom, "Dad...gay? That's impossible! There's no way!"

Christina was nineteen years old, almost twenty. She was old enough to understand what "gay" meant, but not old enough to have a full comprehension of what issues in a person's life may push one in that direction.

Christina was "all girl;" beautiful, thin, shapely, and very interested in the opposite sex. She was fun loving, adorned with a gorgeous and full crop of brunette hair, and she had a girlish, but broad, smile very capable of parting dark and gloomy clouds on a rainy day.

Christi, as most called her, was feisty. She was afraid of no one. She carried herself with a confidence and boldness that had most of the male population close to her very aware of just *"who"* Christina Gil was. All together, these traits had at least twenty young men her age in genuine love with her. Though she had a few gay friends, she did not understand, nor did she accept that her father was also of that orientation.

Furthermore, Christi did not like Daniel. She hadn't been fond of him since the first day her dad brought him home a few weeks before. Now her mother was telling her that her father and this "low life," as she called him, were lovers. She just couldn't accept it. Rejection of the whole idea was her assessment of the situation.

So true was her denial of her mother's report of her dad's homosexuality, it caused her to mentally jettison the whole possibility, and it helped her to fall quickly asleep that night. The next morning, however, she woke up with a resolve. She was going to talk with her dad and straighten the whole thing out once and for all. She called him on his cell phone and reached Daniel.

"Is my father there?" Christi asked forthrightly, ready to lash Daniel to pieces should he show her the slightest resistance.

Daniel said, "Sure Christi, he's right here."

"Can I talk to him?" She snapped back.

"No problem," he responded and handed the phone to Raymond.

"Dad, listen," Christina said abruptly to her father. "Mom told me about you and Daniel, and I don't care about any of it. I just want to talk to you today. Where can we meet? And I don't want Daniel to be there. I want to talk to you alone."

Raymond was beginning to feel the oppressive weight of Daniel's control and wanted to tell Christi about it, but certain factors held him back. First, Daniel was right there listening to Raymond's every word. As well, he didn't want to frighten his daughter. Mostly, however, he feared for his family's safety.

You see by this time, in order to not lose Raymond, Daniel had already begun to control his new arrangement with threats. The exact details of these threats were not known outside the inner circle of Raymond and Daniel. But indeed, they had begun.

Raymond set up a rendezvous with Christi at the parking lot of the apartment complex where he and Daniel were living. She and her dad were going to meet that afternoon just about the same time we were sitting down at the restaurant to have Sunday dinner with our friends.

As we shared joy with old acquaintances, laughing in the liberty of our freedom in Christ; as prevalent as was our freedom—in a parking lot on the other side of town, the bondage of manipulation, deceit, and control taking place between Raymond, Daniel, and Christi was even more prevalent.

When Christi drove up, Raymond was waiting near his van with Daniel at his side. When she saw Daniel standing beside her father, it made her fighting mad, and she slammed her foot down on the gas squealing her tires and sliding the rear of her car as she turned into the lot. She pulled her car to within a few parking places from where they were standing and screeched to a halt. She then exited her vehicle, slammed the door, and walked angrily over to the two men.

Before either of them was able to say a word, Christi demanded, "I want to talk to my father...alone."

Daniel didn't say a word. But his light and cheerful demeanor over the phone from that morning was noticeably gone. He looked at Christi through narrow eyelids and backed up slowly three or four steps—then stopped.

"Would you please leave us alone?" Christi insisted. She glared at Daniel as he glared back at her. He stepped backwards a few more steps but froze there. Defiantly, he folded his arms and positioned himself to move no more.

"Listen, Daniel," Christi said sarcastically, "I am not afraid of you; I don't care how mean or mad you try to look. This is my father, and if I want to talk with him, that's what I am going to do whether you like it or not."

By this time, Raymond was feeling observably uneasy and tried to calm his daughter. He certainly didn't want a fight. Nor did he want Daniel angry or his daughter hurt.

So, trying to distract her from Daniel, Raymond said, "Listen, Christi. Let's just talk."

Christi turned her back abruptly in the direction of Daniel and began talking to her father. But the entire time, Daniel was leaning and inching toward the two of them, trying to catch as much of their conversation as he could.

"Dad," Christi scolded her father, "What is this all about? Don't tell me you are gay, because I know you're not."

Raymond wasn't really focused on answering Christi's questions. He was much more aware of Daniel's presence and concerned that his daughter might say something else to further anger him.

To Christi's surprise, her dad said while looking over her shoulder at Daniel, "No Christina, it really seems like I am. I hope that doesn't disappoint you."

Christina was a little taken aback with his answer, but said, "Well, I still don't believe it. Something isn't right about all this. And what is all this about you divorcing Mom and moving out? I'll support you no matter what you do, but everything is just too weird. Why does Daniel have your phone? Is he forcing you to do any of this?"

By this time, Daniel had crept closer and was now standing within ten feet of Christi and Raymond. Christi suddenly became aware that he had closed the gap between them. She turned in his direction and spouted at him, "Get away from me!"

Daniel didn't move. He stood there in rebellion, and to further intimidate, he looked back at her with dagger-like eyes and folded his arms more emphatically to demonstrate his resistance.

Christi said to him, "I don't know who you think you are, Daniel, but you don't scare me, so don't try."

Just then, Raymond interrupted, "Listen, Christi, it was my choice to leave your mom. Daniel and I are together now. This is the way it is going to be from now on."

Raymond motioned for Daniel to back away, so he backed off.

When Raymond turned back to his daughter, he could see she was crying. He didn't have the presence of mind to be tender to her. He only wanted to get her away from Daniel so she wouldn't enrage him more.

So, Raymond said to Christi in a hurried tone, "Listen, Christi. I love you and everything will be fine. Just go home and tell Mom I will be in touch with her. I have to come to the house later this afternoon to pick up a few more things. If she is there, I'll talk to her then."

Raymond hugged his daughter, who was still in too much shock to hug back. Then he got into the driver's side of his van with Daniel getting in on the opposite side. Christi stood watching as the van's engine started and the vehicle pulled away. Why they were leaving she didn't know since they lived there, but that thought quickly evaporated in the heat of her feelings of consternation, puzzlement, and anger.

Christi was going to meet her boyfriend after that, so she didn't go home following her meeting with her dad. She did feel she wanted to talk to her mom about her encounter with her father but decided she would do that when she arrived home later that night.

After our lunch was over, we went home to prepare for the leadership gathering at the church to take place at six that evening. When we arrived home, Shirley called Sarah to see how she was doing. She told my wife that Raymond had just come over to the house to pick up a few more things. When he came to the door, Daniel was right by his side.

When coming into the front door of the Gil home, there is a small foyer area as you enter. To the right of the foyer is the kitchen. Straight ahead is a double-doorway into the living room and to the left is a hallway leading to the bedrooms.

Sarah told Shirley that when Raymond and Daniel entered, Sarah was in the kitchen. Raymond said, "Sarah, I need to get a few more things." Then he turned to the left and went down the hallway to gather some more of his belongings from their bedroom. Daniel followed Raymond inside and stood in the entryway the same as he had the night before.

The whole time Raymond looked for clothes, Daniel never said a word to Sarah, and she never spoke to him. It struck Sarah though, that Daniel was standing where he was in order to keep her away from Raymond. Her suspicions were strengthened when her husband arrived back in the foyer with his things, because when he did, Daniel walked out the front entrance. Then, while Raymond's back was to the door, he turned to Sarah in the kitchen, and with a shrug of his shoulders, a tilt of his head, and a frustrated look on his face; he seemed to communicate to her, "I'm sorry, but I have no choice." She couldn't be sure, but it caused her to begin to wonder about what kind of influence Daniel might be having upon her husband.

Still in shock, over the phone, Sarah inquired of my wife what she thought she should have done. She asked, "Should I have let Daniel in the door?" She said, "I don't want to antagonize the situation. Should I, as a Christian, be compliant so I don't not push Daniel away from Christ?"

FINALLY ENGAGED

When Shirley hung up the phone, she told me about her conversation with Sarah. As much as it touched me to hear about her sensitivity toward Daniel's spiritual condition, there was something about it that made my blood boil. It was my feeling at that point; that our priority needed to be to save a marriage, and who knows, maybe even a life, before we think about saving a soul. There would be time for salvation discussions later. I also think my disdain for the corruption that was behind this unbelievable Gil family crisis had grabbed my soul. It was from that point that my concern for the situation kicked into high gear.

I knew deep in my heart, though passiveness seemed to have a hold of me earlier that day, that there was no option available to me that would give me permission to not care about Raymond and Sarah. From the moment of my wife's report to me about Sarah's concern for Daniel's soul, I was fully engaged.

I don't think it was that I was unconcerned about Daniel's soul. I think it was that, for the first time, I was alerted to the need for me to care about Sarah's concerns. And Sarah's most vital concern was her husband and her family, and so it was mine.

I also knew from having ministered to Sarah for many years that she had a deep respect for her pastors, whoever they might be, and a simple trust in their leadership. I felt she wanted to trust us and lean on our guidance because she knew we tried as much as we could to take our cues from the Lord. That gave her more peace about trusting us than trusting someone else. As a result, I sensed that she was poised to lean on us. My oath to God to care simply took over at that point.

Our leadership meeting began at six and concluded at eight thirty, after which we went immediately over to the Gils. Their house was less than four blocks from the church. Sarah was waiting for us with a cake she had made.

When we walked into the front door, each of us embraced Sarah compassionately. The three of us sat down at the kitchen table and we began to quiz her concerning how she was doing, while we tried to pick at the cake she had set before us.

Sarah still seemed to be oddly proper and in control. Our appraisal was that she was still in shock. But she did begin to fill us in on the day's activities—a kind of recap since she had already talked to my wife by phone earlier.

As she stirred her coffee, she said, "I'm glad I stayed home from church today, because it gave me a chance to think and get my bearings. This morning early, I went for a walk as I always do. I think it was one of the most uncomfortable and yet necessary walks I have ever taken. I tried not to think much about everything, and when I got home, I felt like my head was clear. But I think that while I was gone, Raymond and Daniel came by the house, because when I walked onto the porch the front door was open and I was sure I had left it closed. Then, when I went into my bedroom to put my sweater away, one of Raymond's shirts was on the bed after I had already made it. Christi must have slept through it with her door closed because she wasn't aware that they had been here."

She continued, "It made me mad because it means they were waiting and watching for me to go on my walk so Raymond could get his things without having to confront me. That frustrated me a little because I wanted to be here when Raymond came so I could talk to him. It also made me uncomfortable because I'm not sure how I feel about Daniel coming into my house. I figure if he would steal my husband, he would steal something else."

Shirley and I listened sympathetically. When she concluded her thought, I asked, "But you did see them again today, didn't you?"

"Yes," She said, "Sometime after Raymond talked to Christina, they came over."

I said, "Wait a minute. Raymond talked to Christina?"

"Yes, Christina called Raymond this morning just after she woke up and set up a meeting with him at the parking lot in front of Daniel's apartment, wherever that is. They talked this afternoon. Christi called me after they met and told me about it, but she hasn't been home, so I don't have all the details. She did tell me enough though to let me know that Raymond's story hasn't changed. He said a lot of the same things to her today that he said to me last night. She did say that Daniel was a nosey jerk. He wouldn't even let them talk alone. I hope to get more information from her when she gets home tonight."

"All right," I said to Sarah. "What happened when Raymond and Daniel came over this afternoon?"

"Well," said Sarah, "They came over and both came into the house. Raymond went into our bedroom to get some more clothes while Daniel stood in the entryway. They were here only a short time, and then they left."

I was steaming mad. The thought of this husband stealer coming into Sarah's house with no reservations really upset me. I had been ready to express my opinion since Shirley told me about her conversation with Sarah earlier.

I asked Sarah, "How do you feel about Daniel coming into your home uninvited, especially since you know he is trying to steal your husband?"

She said, "To be honest, I'm not very comfortable with him being anywhere on our property. But if there is any hope that he might become a Christian, I don't want to cause him to be turned away from the Lord because of my attitude. He can become a Christian, right; I mean even though he is gay?"

My demeanor softened and I said, "Of course he can. Christianity is a 'come as you are faith'. Sarah, when you first came to Christ, were you perfect?"

"No."

"You didn't clean your act up first did you," I asked?

She shook her head no.

"You came as you were, right?"

"Yes." She responded.

"And when you gave your life to Christ were you instantly perfect?" I asked.

"No, not even close."

"That's right none of us were. We were a work in progress right from the beginning. But when we come to Him, he places his Holy Spirit in us and begins to speak to us about the way He wants us to live."

Sarah listened intently and I wondered if she was so engaged for more than one reason; not just for Daniel, but for Raymond.

I continued, "People come to Jesus humbly, as they are. All manner of people do; good people, bad people, straight people, gay people, lesbian people, men and women. It doesn't matter. And when they come, Jesus welcomes them with open arms and places His Holy Spirit in them, what Ephesians calls His seal of ownership, which begins to shape them and change them into His image. We can't change anyone, not even ourselves. Only the Holy Spirit can do that."

I could tell what I was saying was bringing a sense of peace to Sarah.

But then, reverting back to the discomfort I felt before, I said, "Sarah, I commend you for your evangelistic heart and your genuine desire to be a witness for Christ, but I am going to give you permission to treat Daniel with a little more of the righteous indignation I think is inside of you. I do not believe now is the time to think about witnessing for Christ. I am sure there will be ample time for that later. Now is the time to fight for your husband. Do you want him back?"

Sarah responded instantly, "Yes, I do!"

I could tell that was all she needed to hear.

I said, "All right. Listen, Sarah. I think you need to treat Daniel as the thief he is. I think you need to view him as 'the other woman,' the home wrecker bent on destroying your household. My feeling is; he has defiled your home. Furthermore, I think you have every right to tell your husband that you don't want Daniel in your house, on your porch, or for that matter anywhere on your property."

As I told her this, I could see a heavy weight lifting from her. In my mind's eye I could see Sarah rolling up her sleeves and arming herself for battle.

But there was another concern that was weighing on my heart, and that was the total lack of knowledge we had about this man, Daniel Rogers. We didn't know where he came from, or for that matter, anything about him—his background, his character, his upbringing, his family, or his friends. In fact, all we knew for sure was that he was newly out of prison and on parole, and those weren't positive details.

I said, "Sarah, you have every right to stand your ground with Daniel. Treat him as the home destroyer that he is. But I want to caution you, we don't know anything about this guy, and we don't know what he is capable of, so be careful. Tell Raymond you don't want Daniel on your property. Let Raymond deal with it."

We talked for some time about the situation and made some plans for the next day. Mondays were my normal days off; but I could foresee that very little leisure would take place the next day.

No Fear

It was about ten thirty and we were just about ready to leave when Christina arrived home. We had moved from the kitchen to the living room some time during our conversation, and we were just about to pray with Sarah when Christina walked in the door. She didn't stop to converse. She merely offered a formal, "Hello," as she walked by the living room doorway and headed straight down the hall for her bedroom.

Her rigid entrance and cold greeting could have been related to a lot of things; the emotion of the day, shame for what was going on in her family, or even tiredness. But I couldn't help but think it may be related to the coldness I had detected from her concerning the critical issues I knew were in her father's heart and suspected had been transplanted into hers. Just the same, we talked for a few more minutes before I excused myself and went down the hall to look for Christina. I found her in her bedroom. The door was open, so I knocked on the doorframe and asked, "Can I talk to you for a few minutes?"

"Yeah," she said emotionless, shrugging her shoulders. She was sitting on one corner of her bed. I walked in, sat on the other corner, and said "I heard you talked with your father today."

"Yeah, I did," she responded, still without emotion.

I quizzed, "Can I ask what he told you?"

She shrugged again, took a deep breath, and said rather flippantly as if she were simply forwarding information, "He said he was gay and that he and Daniel were going to be a couple now."

She was trying to sound matter of fact, but I could feel the pain within her seeping out of every pore. I paused for a few moments, allowing time for myself to think through my next words before I said, "How did that make you feel?"

"Well, I guess he can do whatever he wants. He's a grown man," she said coldly.

I persisted in my interrogation despite the coldness I felt, "Did you get to talk to your dad alone without Daniel around?"

With this question I seemed to trigger a response.

Christi looked at me and said, "Just so you know, I still don't think my father is gay. And Daniel doesn't scare me." Then she stood, took a step toward her dresser and began to fidget with some things on its top.

I knew she was in great pain, both from the whole situation and maybe even having to talk with me, but not just because it was me. She probably didn't want to talk to anyone about what she perceived to be a hard to understand probability concerning her father.

When Christi expressed her lack of fear of Daniel, I knew I needed to say the same thing to her as I had said to Sarah. So, I cautioned, "Christi, I don't know how much contact you will have with Daniel, but I think I need to warn you to be careful with him. We don't know anything about him, and we don't know what he is capable of."

Christina responded, "I understand what you are saying, but you just need to know, I am not afraid of him."

I couldn't tell if her obstinacy was due to a resistance to me, a naiveté about life or some intimidation she was still feeling from Daniel that afternoon. I knew Christi to be very strong willed. Perhaps her desire to portray herself as fearless was nothing more than a power struggle between her and Daniel. Whatever it was, I didn't feel the freedom to pursue the subject any further.

I said, "Well, Shirley and I are available if you need to talk, and we'll keep in touch with your mom. If you need anything, feel free to call us any time or tell your mom and she'll get a hold of us. OK?"

"OK," she said, and I left to go back into the living room.

Shirley and Sarah were wrapping up their conversation, and I gathered them together to pray. Just before I began, Christina walked by and into the kitchen, so we invited her to join us. We all held hands in the Gil living room and prayed for Raymond's safety, God's will for the situation, a miracle for the Gil family, and, yes, even for Daniel's salvation.

That was Day Two.

DAY THREE
MONDAY

The phone rang midway through the morning on Monday. It was Sarah. On separate receivers Shirley and I talked to her for more than an hour.

She began the conversation, "I think there are some other things going on. I think Daniel is controlling Raymond."

Up until this point, the idea that Daniel was manipulating and exercising power over Raymond had only been slightly considered. Sarah had alluded to a suspicion she had about this on Saturday night, and we knew Daniel was reluctant to leave Raymond's side, but there was no evidence to suggest that Raymond's decision to leave Sarah was anything more than his own willing choice.

Honestly, when Sarah first suggested idea of control, I wondered if it was just a hopeful cry from a desperate wife simply wanting all of it to "not be so." However, as Sarah began to analyze all that had happened up until then, it seemed to her that Raymond was not at all himself when Daniel was around.

She began to describe her observations to us on the phone that Monday morning.

"Like on Saturday night after the dinner," Sarah said, "I didn't think much about it then, but the whole time Raymond seemed to be looking at Daniel before he spoke as if he was trying to get an OK from him. Then, after they got back from Daniel's apartment, Raymond was glancing nonstop over at Daniel. Besides that, when Raymond talked, Daniel didn't look at me, out the window, or at the floor. He looked at Raymond, not supportively, but like he was monitoring his every word. I thought this was odd at the time, but I didn't know why."

Sarah went on, "After you left last night, I talked to Christi about her conversation with her father that afternoon. She said Daniel couldn't keep his nose out of her conversation with Raymond. She told me it was like he had to hear everything they were saying. Then, when Christi was talking to Raymond with her back to Daniel, he tried to wedge himself into the conversation. But here is the weird part: Raymond didn't get in Daniel's face. That's not like Raymond at all. If Raymond thought anyone was trying to hurt his daughter, he would be all over the person. Christi told me that when she was talking with her dad, Raymond was like a peacemaker. He seemed afraid and was trying to appease Daniel. It didn't seem right to her and it doesn't seem right to me either. That's not like Raymond, at least, not when it comes to his daughter."

Shirley and I listened intently. I was beginning to feel great concern for the whole situation. I wasn't sure whether Daniel was controlling Raymond. But I felt if he was; it would complicate the already delicate situation considerably.

Sarah continued, "Yesterday I called Raymond a few times to ask him some questions. I also received a call from him telling me when he was going to come by to pick up his belongings. But when I talk to him, he doesn't seem right. Raymond and I have had our problems and haven't been the best spouses to each other over the years, but I am close enough to him to know when he is being himself and when he isn't."

"Every time he calls me, it doesn't sound like him. I mean it is, but it is like Daniel is right beside him controlling his every word, making sure he says all the correct things. I don't know much, but I know my husband, and he is not himself. Yesterday, when he and Daniel came by to get more of Raymond's things, Daniel went out the door first. When he did, Raymond looked at me, and the look he gave me made me think something isn't right. Daniel must be twisting his arm or trying to make him say 'uncle' or something."

I thought Sarah may have been trying to read things into the story just a bit, so I said, "You might be right, Sarah, but remember, this whole situation is different. Maybe Raymond is acting different because this is all different for him or he is ashamed in front of you."

Sarah responded, "Well, maybe, but listen to this. I went on my walk later than usual this morning. I wanted to change my time, because Raymond knows when I usually go. I wanted to be sure they didn't come to the house for some more of Raymond's things while I was walking like they did yesterday."

"While I was away, Raymond called me from the dentist's office and left a message. I knew he had an appointment this morning, but I had forgotten. On our answer machine, he left a message as though he was trying to talk very fast, and he said, 'I can't talk long. Daniel went outside to have a cigarette, so I am calling you on the phone here at the dentist's office. Daniel has my cell phone and won't let me out of his sight. Every time I call you, he is right beside me with his ear to the phone, so I can't say what I want to say. I can only say what I feel will be safe to say and what he wants me to say.'"

Sarah went on, "And I think Daniel is threatening Raymond. Something Raymond said on the answer machine makes me think that. You see, Chris," Sarah pleaded, "I can tell the difference between Raymond's voice when Daniel is with him and when he's not. I don't need to see them together. I know."

It was starting to look like we were into something we were quite unprepared to deal with. After Shirley and I hung up with Sarah, I tried to recall my impressions of Daniel when I met him at church a few weeks before.

Raymond had told me the week prior that he was bring-ing a friend to church, someone he had hired in his business. I remember Raymond telling me that his friend was a little nervous about church, so I shouldn't ask him many questions, because it might scare him away.

On that Sunday I met Daniel in the church kitchen before the service. We always make refreshments available at that time. Sarah saw me enter the room and brought Daniel over to introduce him to me. When introductions were stated, I simply reached out my hand to shake his, and he reached out his to shake mine.

I said smiling, "Hi, Daniel. Good to meet you." And he said back to me, "Good to meet you, too." And that was it.

I thought hard, but there were no tell-tale signs of mental illness, psychotic behavior, or criminal tendencies. His face possessed a hard look such as I had observed on faces over the years of those who had led difficult lives. But there was noth-ing to indicate that he was any more dangerous than anyone else, and at the time he came to church, I didn't know he was on parole. Yet, as I sat there, I determined it might be wise if I at least called law enforcement to see if there was anything they could do to help in the situation.

I grabbed the phone and called the police, hoping to talk to someone about our predicament. I told the receptionist without mentioning their name a little about the dilemma with the Gil family and that it might be a dangerous situation. I was a little disappointed that all I was able to do was leave a message for an officer to call me back when he became free.

FIRE IN HER EYES

Meanwhile, Sarah was dealing with Raymond and Daniel. It seems midway through the day they came by the house so Raymond could pick up some more things. When they pulled into the driveway, Daniel thought he would accompany

Raymond into the house as he had before. But when he walked onto the front porch and attempted to come in through the door, Sarah met both he and Raymond before they could enter. Sarah had her proverbial claws extended and her teeth bared. As she confronted them, she used all the terminology and planning we had discussed with her the night before.

She said boldly and angrily to Raymond plenty loud enough for Daniel to hear, "Raymond, I don't want that man in my house. I don't want him on our porch or anywhere on our property. He is the other woman trying to steal my husband. He is nothing more than a home wrecker, and he has defiled our house. I want him out of here, now!" Her approach wasn't exactly what I had recommended, but it got her point across. She didn't even look at Daniel. She kept her gaze on Raymond, so she couldn't see Daniel's reaction. But Daniel was livid. Raymond didn't know what to say, but it terrified him. He looked at Daniel, recognized the disdain on his face, and knew he needed to act fast. Raymond started trying to gently coax Daniel back away from the door. But Daniel's dynamite temper had been ignited.

Over Raymond's shoulder and aimed at Sarah, he retorted, "I'll go where I want. This is Raymond's house too you know, and he wants me, not you."

However, Sarah was not going to be intimidated. From the door she added a final dig. With Raymond's back to her, as he was still trying to back Daniel off the porch and toward the van, Sarah spouted, "Raymond, if he comes onto our property again, I'll call the police."

When she said that, the look on Daniel's face immediately changed from anger to fear, and Daniel backed right away. No one had given it any thought until then, but Daniel knew; one questionable encounter with the police, because of his "parole" status, could land him back in jail in a flash. So, he became compliant rather quickly. He didn't leave the property completely though. He moved to the rear of the van and paced nervously. From there he demanded, "Raymond, you better get your things and hurry up."

Raymond scurried back to the front porch and into the house. Sarah was waiting at the door and stepped aside as Raymond entered. He stopped only for a split second as he passed her and looked straight into her eyes in a way that seemed to plead, "I'm so sorry for all this, but there's nothing I can do about it."

Don't ask me how she could gather all that from a look, but she felt certain that is what his glance meant.

Raymond then moved quickly down the hall to their bedroom.

Sarah thought about following Raymond to ask him any question that might shed more light on the whole mess, but the confusion level in her brain was still off the charts. She wasn't sure if she should, or could, or really wanted to. The only thought that came to her mind that had any clarity at all was...*watch Daniel to make sure he stays behind the van.* So, she moved from the entryway into the kitchen in front of the sink where she could see more clearly out the window.

She could hear Raymond rummaging through the bedroom closet and then the bathroom drawers, but her mind wouldn't allow her to form thoughts about what she might say to her husband. It was only focused on her enemy, the husband-stealer behind the van.

And then she sensed Raymond looking at her from the foyer as he had apparently finished his hunt for toiletries and such. He was staring at his wife, waiting for her to look back at him from her post in front of the kitchen window. He was standing in a position that would allow Sarah to see him, but not Daniel if Daniel happened to be looking toward the front door.

When Sarah turned to look, Raymond whispered loud enough for her to hear, "Sarah, I love *you*. I love *you!*" He then paused long enough and looked into her eyes until he was sure she understood.

Raymond then leaned toward the door to leave, but Sarah stopped him.

That morning when Sarah got up, since she didn't go on her usual early morning walk, she used the time to read the Bible. She had also taken time to comb through its pages to find as many scriptures as she could. She had written them down on a single piece of paper, hoping Raymond would come by the house again so she could give them to him.

She said, "Raymond, just stay right there." She then hurried into the TV room, which was off the opposite end of the kitchen, grabbed the piece of paper, and hurried back to where Raymond was, folding it into as small a package as she could on the way. She gave it to him and said, "Here, put these scriptures in your pocket. Look at them later."

Raymond stuffed them into his pocket and nodded appreciatively. He then slipped quickly out the door. As Sarah moved back in front of the kitchen window, Raymond and Daniel climbed into the van and drove off.

After they were out of sight, Sarah continued to stare straight ahead and out the window for several moments. She couldn't see the large trees in front of the house, their shaggy un-mowed front yard, their silver Ford in the driveway, the street passing in front of their home, falling leaves, flying birds, the houses across the street, or anything within the scope of her gaze. All she could see was Raymond saying, "Sarah, I love *you*. I love *you*. I love *you*." He had whispered the words, but as she stood in front of her kitchen window, she heard them echoing, reverberating, shouting loudly in her mind.

For years she had longed for her husband to say those words to her. She could barely remember the last time he spoke them; and even further from her recollection was him saying them to her and meaning them at the same time. That day she heard him say them in a setting where she was forced to consider that he really might have meant them; but it was perplexing because she really wasn't sure how she felt about it.

Just the same, the words kept echoing in her mind. As she stood staring out the window, oblivious to her surroundings and playing back in her head the tape of those words over and over again, she knew one thing for sure. She wasn't positive how she felt about her husband or their marriage, their future or their family; but she was certain Raymond was not solely responsible for the decisions he had been making since Saturday night.

It was at that point Sarah truly began to fear for Raymond's safety. She was now convinced that what she had told me that morning was indeed true. If Raymond's whispered words meant anything, at the very least they meant her husband wasn't in full control of his life.

She reasoned, "If Raymond loved her and not Daniel, then why was he still with Daniel?"

POLICE

The phone ringing broke her concentration. She answered it and sat down at the kitchen table. I was phoning her to let her know I had called the police to obtain information from them, but they hadn't yet called back. That is when she informed me of what had just happened.

Sarah asked me, "Are you sure we need to call them? Do you think," she further questioned, "If Daniel is pressuring Raymond to do and say certain things, that it might make things worse? Besides, I'm not sure how Christi would feel about our calling the police. I thought about it last night and mentioned the possibility to her, but she said she didn't think it was that serious. Before we call them, I would like to get her permission. She is our daughter, and I believe we need to include her in these decisions."

I understood what she was saying, but I felt as though we did need to at least seek advice from someone in law enforcement, especially after the encounter she had just had with her husband and Daniel.

We decided that when I talked to an officer, rather than give him the names of all those involved, I would just describe the situation to him and ask what he would advise. Sarah felt OK with that, at least until she could talk to Christina. I hung up with Sarah, so I could wait for the return call from the police department.

Late that afternoon the phone rang at our house. It was a city police detective. He told me he was an officer in training but would try to help. My first thought was, *Great. We got the trainee.* But I told him about the situation just the same, leaving the names out of the mix.

He said, "First, we can't do anything unless we talk to the wife. Then, we can't really approach the husband unless we can get permission directly from him."

Well, I wasn't quite sure what to do. I knew getting permission from Raymond was going to be touchy. It seemed as if Daniel had control of Raymond's phone. If Daniel did let Raymond talk on it, it was apparent that Daniel had his ear to the receiver listening to the caller's every word and affecting Raymond's responses. Even if we were able to pose the right question to Raymond, and he wanted to say yes, would Daniel hear and influence Raymond to say the opposite? If that happened, where would we be then?

I told the officer I would speak to the wife and ask her if she would consider calling him. He told me he would be getting off his shift at eight that night, but if she called, he would talk to her immediately. I hung up with him and called Sarah.

By this time, it was about five in the afternoon. When Sarah answered, I discussed with her what I believed to be the importance of working with the police as opposed to trying to handle the situation on our own. She was reluctant, because she was afraid if the situation weren't as serious as we thought it might be; it would really anger Raymond to have the police, and therefore the whole city involved.

"First," I told Sarah, "The police have authority to do things we do not. They may be able to scare Daniel because of his parole and cause him to back off, but we don't have that leverage without them. They may find Daniel is in violation of his parole right now. Maybe his threats to Raymond are a parole violation, and they will take him and put him in jail immediately and that will be the end of that."

Most importantly, I told her, "The whole situation just seems to be potentially dangerous for your whole family, and it might be foolish for us to *not* include law enforcement."

After several minutes of discussion, I was able to convince Sarah, but she still felt she needed to secure Christi's permission first. She told me Christi should be coming home soon and she would ask her.

By seven, I still hadn't heard from Sarah, so I called her to see what was up. Just as I began to speak to her, she told me Christi was pulling into the driveway. I asked Sarah if I could speak to her.

When she came to the phone, I said, "Christi, I know you aren't in complete agreement with our talking to the police about this, but your mom and I think there are some control issues going on between Daniel and your dad that aren't right. Besides, I am beginning to sense, and your mom now agrees, this whole thing may be more dangerous than any of us had originally thought. I still think we need to consider what I told you last night at your house. We don't know anything about this man, and we don't know what he is capable of."

Christi listened, and I could tell she wasn't in full agreement, but I think better sense got the best of her, and she responded, "Well, I still don't think it is really that big of a deal. I told you, I'm not afraid of Daniel. But if Mom thinks we should call the police, then that is her choice."

I said, "Yes, Christi, but your mom wants you to agree with it before we would do it."

Christi responded, "OK then. Fine! Call the police."

Sarah got back on the phone. I told her to go ahead and call the officer I had talked to earlier that day and to call me afterward to let me know what he said.

MOTHER AND DAUGHTER

Sarah is an incredible lady. Since she received Christ into her life many years earlier, she has been in deep love with God. She claims Jesus as her Savior and tells most people she meets about her relationship with Him. No one who knows her well would ever doubt the genuineness of her walk with the Lord. Furthermore, she is always inviting people who are not believers to come to church with the hope that they would hear the gospel and decide for Christ. She doesn't at all feel her efforts to talk to people infringes on their privacy. She believes strongly in the command of Jesus to witness. To not share with someone who isn't a Christian would be a clear act of disobedience to His great commission in Matthew 28. That is just the way she feels.

Sarah's priority, however, has always been her daughter. Above all else, she wanted Christina to know the Lord. At times, Sarah was a bit overbearing in her zeal to see Christi become a Christian, because there were times, she would push a little too hard, or hint a little too strongly, or remind a little too often, leaving Christi rolling her eyes at her mom's preaching. But it was all because Sarah loved her little girl and truly believed she needed to have her own living relationship with the Lord if she was going to spend eternity in heaven.

That is why Sarah didn't want to decide about contacting the police in Raymond's situation without first seeking Christina's agreement. She wanted her daughter to know her mother valued her input. It was just a part of Sarah's longing to see her daughter become a Christian.

After I hung up with Sarah, I waited another two hours for her to phone me back, but she never did. At nine-fifteen that night, I finally called her thinking she must have forgotten to call me after talking to the police.

When she answered to my chagrin, she said, "I called the officer right after I talked to you, you know, about seven thirty or so, but he wasn't available. So, I left a message for him to call me back, but I haven't heard from him yet."

Deep in my heart, sheltered from Sarah's ears, there was a frustration brewing, which was aimed at the police department, not because of their failure to respond, but because of the growing concern I was beginning to have for the Gil family.

I told Sarah they were probably occupied by other pressing matters and would no doubt call her either later tonight or first thing in the morning. But when they called, I wanted her to inquire about two things. The first was a restraining order against Daniel. It seemed to me his words to her that day could possibly be interpreted as harassment and qualify for that kind of an order to be granted. I also told her to ask about how significant it was that Daniel was on parole. I wanted to know how possible it was that they could just take him away, lock him up, and get him out of our hair once and for all. After going over these concerns with Sarah, I prayed with her and we hung up.

When our phone receivers hit their respective cradles, I sat down to relax from a stressful day off. Sarah walked down the hall to talk to her daughter.

"Christi?" she asked, "How do you really feel about all this? What do you think about your father? Are you angry with him? Do you still love him? Are you sure you are OK with us calling the police?" All these questions made up their discussion.

Sarah talked to Christina for nearly an hour that night, primarily about what their family was going through that week. And this night, she started feeling and believing that through this time, her daughter would be drawn closer to the Lord.

That was Day Three.

DAY FOUR
TUESDAY

Over the years I have had emergency situations occupy my time for two or three days, but never up to a week. I wasn't sure how long this event would go on, but I had the feeling it wouldn't resolve itself quickly. My concern over this simply had to do with getting my work done. I knew very well what it would take to put together my sermon and the other logistics for the upcoming Sunday.

Upon arriving at church on this morning, I was resolved to plunge into my sermon, but something was nagging at me. I couldn't figure out why I had not been able to foresee these gay tendencies in Raymond.

In every church I had led as pastor, I had members who struggled with their sexual orientation. Some of them also had personalities and upbringings like that of Raymond, causing inclinations in the direction of gayness. Yet with Raymond, I was never able to detect any of it, and I couldn't figure out why.

As I thought on it that day, I wondered: *Was it because of his gruff demeanor? Was it his tendency to point legalistically at the sins and failures of others? Was I blinded by my own frustration with Raymond? Did I have a greater ignorance of the gay lifestyle than I thought?* Truthfully, I didn't know, and neither did my wife. She had counseled Raymond and was aware of some of his upbringing issues and the animosity he held toward his father, but she hadn't foreseen it either.

There was another question puzzling me on this morning. Where was Sarah getting her desire to help her husband, better yet, keep him? I knew about the power of Christ to impress upon His people a motivation to forgive, but this situation seemed like it spilled over into the "unpardonable sin" category, at least for spouses in marriages. It didn't, of course, but it seemed that way. It caused me to wonder from where Sarah was drawing her will to go after her husband to win him back.

I knew of other situations where women were married to men who later confessed to being gay. There was no restoration to be found in any of the marriages because the husbands had no sexual desire for their wives. The scenario with Sarah and Raymond seemed very similar. I knew God's love was great, but I had my doubts that in the end the Gil marriage would be able to weather this storm.

There were three very good reasons for this.

First, it seemed there was little, or no love being shared between Raymond and Sarah. They were at each other's throats most of the time, and the lack of desire in their sexual relationship was more than just related to impotence. There was loathing going on.

Second, it was also apparent Raymond had little, if any, love for God. In addition, prior to this event, Sarah had confessed to my wife she felt very little love for Raymond. She wanted their marriage to work but wasn't optimistic even before the gay issue surfaced. How could a marriage survive with so little love existing between partners, or for God, where Raymond was concerned?

Third, I also knew that as soon as family, friends, and the church learned of this bizarre turn of events in the Gil family, Sarah would be inundated with people advising her to "drop the bum." *In the natural*, I just couldn't see how the two of them could stay together; and I was seeing very little hope *in the spiritual* as well.

When I came to from my daydream, I shed my wandering imaginations and zeroed in on my sermon for Sunday. But the thoughts continued to nag at me.

I only worked a short time before the other side of pastoral responsibility gripped my heart and I realized I hadn't yet touched bases with Sarah that morning. I put down my pen and dialed their number. No answer concerned me. I left word for Sarah on her answer machine to return my call when she retrieved mine, then I slipped back into my work.

POLICE DEPARTMENT

In the meantime, Sarah was unwilling to wait any longer for a return call from the detective with whom she had left a message the night before. Just prior to my phone call, she had called the police department and asked to talk to another officer on duty. She described the entire story to him from Saturday night up until that moment.

She told him about the control with which she feared Daniel Rogers was oppressing her husband, and that she feared for his safety. She also inquired as to whether Daniel's parole status would have any bearing on the situation and about the possibility of taking out a restraining order. This officer was also uncertain about a few things, but he was considerably more helpful than the detective I spoke with the previous night.

Concerning trying to contact Raymond to find out how severely he was being controlled by Daniel, this officer also maintained there was nothing they could do unless Raymond called them and requested police assistance. From my experience in working with the police in the past, I felt there was something else they could do, but I didn't know exactly what.

As far as Daniel's parole was concerned, the officer told Sarah he could not be arrested unless it could be determined that he was indeed threatening to harm Raymond, her, or Christina. He did agree with our suggestion that Sarah should come down to the police station and take out a restraining order against Daniel. He verified that what happened between Sarah and Daniel the day before did constitute harassment and was enough to justify pulling a restraining order. That way, if he ever did come onto their property after that, he could be arrested for violating the order and therefore his parole. He told Sarah, however, it would take a few days, probably until Thursday or Friday, to have it processed and then served.

After talking with the officer, Sarah called a friend from our church and asked the person to go with her to police headquarters to take out the restraining order. She filled out the necessary paperwork and put her name on it as the person to be protected. That is where she was when I called. When she returned home, she called me to fill me in.

By the time Sarah phoned me, I was well into my sermon. She reported to me all the police officer had said. After some discussion, we were still at a loss as to how to get Raymond alone so we could confirm our suspicions about the control we felt was going on. Nor did we have any certainties about what Raymond's reaction would be to our getting the police involved. We both resolved that Sarah just needed to wait for Raymond to call or come by the house and hope for the right moment to talk with him. I prayed with Sarah and went back to my work.

THE PLOT

Apparently, in one of Raymond's short phone calls to Sarah, when Daniel was away smoking a cigarette, Raymond threw out a suggestion. His idea was for me to meet him in the back room of his chiropractor's office so he could talk to someone without Daniel listening. But before he was able to give details, Daniel returned, and he had to hang up. It was this catalyst that prompted Sarah to call and talk to me a few hours later about a notion she had for getting to talk to Raymond.

Sarah remembered that after work most Tuesdays, Raymond stopped off at his chiropractor's office in a nearby city for his weekly adjustment. This chiropractor was a friend of the Gils, and he might allow someone to hide out in the back room and wait for the two men to show up for Raymond's weekly visit.

If they did come, Daniel would have to stay in the waiting room while Raymond went into the adjustment room for his treatment. If someone were in the back, that person could pass Raymond a note or talk quickly and quietly to him. If that could happen, perhaps we could gain the information we needed for the police without Daniel even knowing.

Sarah asked, "Would you be able to help with this."

"Of course," I said, and we talked for a few more minutes making plans.

There were several things we needed to secure from Raymond.

We needed to obtain his and Daniel's address. We knew what building they were living in, but not the exact number of their apartment.

In addition, we needed to acquire clarification as to whether Daniel was manipulating Raymond with threats.

Last, we needed to give Raymond the phone number of the police department, as well as the name of the detective to talk to so he could call and request an intervention.

We also needed to tell him about the restraining order Sarah had taken out on Daniel. We laid out our strategies and concluded our conversation.

After hanging up with Sarah, I took a big breath and called the doctor. It was about two thirty in the afternoon. When he answered, I identified myself and began my explanation: "Raymond and Sarah are in a severe crisis. I am calling you at Sarah's request to see if you would be able to help."

He was noticeably taken aback, but he and his wife were friends with the Gils, and so naturally, he was concerned.

"What kind of help?" he asked.

I wanted to describe the situation with enough information to impress upon him the urgency of the matter, but not with so much information that it would go beyond what Sarah might say if she were talking to him. I told him about Raymond's relationship with Daniel but tried to make it seem more like control on Daniel's part than a gay orientation on Raymond's. I told him about our inability to talk with Raymond alone and what the police had said about needing to talk to Raymond before they could intervene.

I said, "That is where you come in. Sarah wants me to come to your office around five tonight. Since Raymond usually comes on Tuesday between five and six, she wants me to wait in your back room for them to come. Assuming Daniel is with him as we suspect he will be, when you take Raymond into the adjustment room, close the door and I will communicate the things to Raymond he needs to know. What do you think?"

He said, "Of course I want to help, but how dangerous is this guy?" It was a good and fair question, one we had been asking ourselves. But I had to chuckle to myself.

This chiropractor was a massive man. He stood at least six and a half feet tall, maybe more, and weighed no less than three hundred pounds. And he wasn't all flab. He was solid. But his apprehension spoke of the concern we all had. How dangerous was Daniel? Even the chiropractor's size wasn't impervious to the right weapon in the hands of a dangerous man.

I resisted smiling and said, "I don't really know. But the police won't get involved until they have certain information from Raymond. Sarah can't do it alone, so she is asking for our help. I'm sure she will understand if you feel uncomfortable with the whole thing."

In the end he agreed, with noticeable hesitation, but wanted to check with Sarah before he gave his final consent. I told him to call me if after talking to Sarah he changed his mind. If not, then I would be at his office a little before five that evening to go over details and get situated for "Operation Talk to Raymond."

I arrived at about quarter to five. We discussed details, turned the office music up a little to cover conversation, manned our positions with the chiropractor in the front and myself in the back, and we waited.

We didn't talk during that time, because he felt he needed to stay up front near his office in case Raymond and Daniel happened to slip in without our seeing them. That way, we would not arouse their suspicions by hustling into position at the last minute. So, we waited quietly in separate rooms.

We waited until six, the doctor's closing time, but Daniel and Raymond never showed. Consequently, I helped him close-down and we abandoned the plan, at least for that day.

After he locked the door, we stood in front of his office talking for a few minutes. I thanked him for his willingness to help and assured him either Sarah or myself would let him know how things were developing. Then I gave him a hug and walked toward my car.

As I was about to enter my driver's side door, the doctor got my attention to tell me, "When Raymond doesn't come on Tuesdays, he almost always comes the next day, but usually in the early afternoon."

I told him I would tell Sarah and we would talk about our options. Then we parted.

WHAT TO DO?

When I arrived home, I called Sarah to let her know of our foiled plan. She hadn't heard from Raymond either. We were both somewhat baffled about what we might try next. As we talked, Sarah shared with me a concern she had. It seemed to her that since her confrontation with Daniel the day before, Raymond's communication with her had diminished considerably. That worried Sarah, because if there was anything she didn't want, it was less contact with Raymond. And she was wondering whether she had done the right thing by confronting Daniel as she did.

I assured her that approaching Daniel probably didn't affect Raymond's desire to call her. Instead, it most likely scared Daniel, and we wanted Daniel back on his heels rather than in control.

I tried to help Sarah see that her efforts to set clear boundaries to protect her home had also taken some control away from Daniel, and that was a good thing. Although there was a strong possibility it had made Raymond a little nervous, we would probably hear from him soon. I also told her what the chiropractor had said about Raymond's habit of coming to his office the next afternoon when he missed on Tuesdays. I told her to let me know if she would like me to help connect with Raymond the next day. She said she would think about it.

By this time, others besides the chiropractor were finding out about what was going on with the Gils. The person who had taken Sarah to the police department that morning had told some others and Sarah had told a few people. So, she was receiving calls from folks seeking the gossipy details, expressing their condolences, and unfortunately, offering their suggestions about what she should do with her husband.

She was already hearing, "Leave him." "If he wants men, let him have men." "Why put yourself through the grief." "He deserves whatever he gets."

As we wound down our phone call, Sarah's question to me that night after hearing all the voices expressing their opinions to her was, "Pastor, what do you think I should do?"

It was a loaded question if I had ever heard one. I have had people ask me this kind of question with abundant regularity over the years in the ministry about various things. Sometimes I think I know exactly what they should do. Sometimes I am not so sure. But always, it has been my conviction it was my job to help them discover for themselves what God would have them to do, which is usually rather simple. But never-before had the role of helping someone discover God's will for them been so difficult a task as when Sarah asked me her question. This was largely because I was quite foggy myself about what God and His Word would have to say to her.

I said, "Sarah, you need to look into your own heart. What do you think you should do? Even more important, what do you think God would have you to do?"

Sarah responded to my question, "Well, some of the people who talked to me today make a good point, and most of them are really good Christians. So, I guess I shouldn't just discount what they feel. Doesn't the Bible say that there is much wisdom in many counselors?"

"My first reaction is," she went on, "I need to stick by Raymond until I know he is safe and until I know the truth about how he feels about me. I mean, how would I feel if I dumped him now and something awful happened to him from all this. I don't think I would feel good at all. I think I would feel really bad, and I'm not sure I would ever be able to forgive myself."

Listening to Sarah, I marveled. She sounded more righteous than I. Her thinking was: *She could follow her friend's advice . . . or . . . she could let her friends think her a fool and follow her heart to stand by her man*, which she believed was what God was leading her to do.

I said, "Sarah, personally, it would be a very difficult decision for me. But as you describe what you are feeling, I think what you said is right. I feel you are thinking in a way that would be pleasing to God, especially since we may be Raymond's only advocates."

Certainly, some of the people who are advising you don't care enough about Raymond to want to save his life right now. It isn't that they want him to crash and burn. They are probably reacting the way they are to protect you, and they may change their minds in time. But at this crucial point, Raymond needs someone with your kind of unconditional loyalty. Without it, he could be in serious trouble. We don't know for sure what kind of danger he is in, but until we do, I think your heart to help your husband may be God's plan for Raymond right now." After a few more minutes we hung up.

MOTHER-DAUGHTER TALK # TWO

Sarah waited up for Christina, hoping to get an opportunity to talk to her daughter. She didn't have to wait for long. Christina came home much earlier than usual. When she came into the house, her mom was sitting in the living room in sight of the front door, so Christi came in to converse with her.

As Christina sat down beside Sarah, she asked, "Mom, have you heard from Daddy today?"

"Not really," responded Sarah. "Just a phone call earlier this morning, but I missed it."

Christina didn't say anything right away. Instead, she stared thoughtfully into her own lap for several moments. Sarah saw her thinking, so she didn't interrupt. She just waited for her to speak.

"Mom," Christina finally said, "Are you doing all right?"

"I'm doing surprisingly well," Sarah responded. "God has to be helping me."

As she looked at her daughter, she thought she sensed something she hadn't seen in many months, perhaps years. Sarah thought she detected tenderness and a concern for her mother. She hoped it was so and wondered if that was the reason Christina came home early.

In response to Christina's apparent interest in her welfare, Sarah began talking about the events of that day. She told her daughter about the restraining order and my unproductive visit to the chiropractor's office. She told her about the phone calls from her dad's "not so sympathetic" supporters and her conversation with me about what she should do concerning her support of Raymond.

Sarah also asked Christina what she thought her mom should do.

Christina said, "Mom, you need to decide for yourself. But he's my daddy, and you're my mom. I don't want anything to happen to Daddy, and it scares me to think what will happen to you and our family if you get divorced."

Sarah and Christina talked in that way for over an hour.

In short, they had their second mother-daughter talk of the week, this one even tenderer than the last. Afterward, they prayed together again for Christina's daddy.

That was Day Four.

DAY FIVE
WEDNESDAY

If there was a reprieve for me from intensity in the Gil crisis, it took place on this day. My call to Sarah early that day only received an answer machine, on which I left a message. I did not receive a return call from Sarah until much later that evening. It was then that she presented me with a report of the day's happenings.

It could be Sarah sensed I needed to focus on my work and decided to give me the day off. I am sure she also felt bad that I had gone to the trouble of trying to connect with Raymond at the chiropractor's office the day before with no results. So, Sarah chose to handle Wednesday by herself. For her there was no reprieve from the stress of the last four days.

Sarah received a call from Raymond in the first part of the morning. It was a controlled call. She could tell Daniel was leaning his ear in the direction of the receiver, so she wasn't able to talk freely with her husband. Sarah, however, was somewhat shrewd herself and by then had thought the situation through enough—and had become desperate enough—to do some manipulating of her own.

Sarah was a hairdresser and operated a business out of her home. Raymond was phoning to inform his wife of a call he had taken the previous week from a lady who wanted Sarah to cut her hair on Wednesday. He knew he had told his wife but was using this as an opportunity to connect with Sarah. He remembered, because the whole incident had prompted a huge fight between him and his wife when he had forgotten to write down the lady's name.

Raymond had said deceptively to Daniel, "I have to call Sarah, because she won't be expecting the lady for an appointment this afternoon." So, Daniel conceded.

Raymond knew he had told her and was pretty sure she would remember the incident, but he also hoped she would be alert enough to play along with his little ploy.

When Sarah answered the phone, Raymond said in a formal voice, "Hi, Sarah. Listen, I'm just calling to let you know some lady called last week to make a hair appointment for today. I wasn't sure whether I had told you about it. I know it is late notice, but the appointment is for two o'clock this afternoon, and I wanted to let you know so you could be ready for it."

Indeed, she was very alert to what Raymond was attempting to do but didn't want to let on that she knew. She had actually cancelled that appointment, as well as all her appointments that week in light of her pending crisis but didn't feel it was necessary to communicate that to Raymond right then.

Instead, she answered in an equally formal manner, "Well, thank you, Raymond. I'm not sure whether you told me about it or not. But she called yesterday to confirm, so I was aware of the appointment."

She continued in a regimented tone, "By the way, Raymond, did you remember to go to the chiropractor yesterday? You know you usually have back trouble if you don't."

Of course, Sarah knew he hadn't gone, and from our conversation the night before, she knew if he didn't go on Tuesdays, he almost always went on Wednesdays. But she was fishing for information hoping Raymond would confirm he was indeed going to be paying his doctor a visit that afternoon.

Raymond had no idea what Sarah was up to, and so ignorantly he played along saying, "No, I couldn't go yesterday.

We had to work late, and I couldn't get there on time. I need to go today, though. We have to cut off early, so I'm sure I'll get there sometime this afternoon."

"OK, and doesn't he close his office a little early on Wednesdays?"

Before Raymond could answer though, Sarah said, "Raymond, if there is nothing else, I have to go now. I have some things I need to do."

Raymond, a little surprised at Sarah's glibness, said tentatively, "OK. Good-bye, I guess."

Raymond was noticeably shaken by what seemed to be Sarah's lack of desire to talk with him more. It wasn't as if there was much more they could say with Daniel beside him listening to every word, but it made him wonder if she had crossed a line of disgust and decided to let him go his own way.

He didn't share his concern with Daniel, but deep in his heart the whole conversation made him feel extremely uneasy. He had been clinging to the hope his wife would still have him. He was also very afraid of Daniel and saw Sarah as his only possible source of deliverance. He felt that if Sarah quit talking to him, who else would?

Sarah, however, had two reasons for talking to Raymond the way she did and cutting off their conversation so abruptly.

First, she didn't want to arouse suspicion in Daniel. She wanted him feeling as relaxed as possible about his and Raymond's relationship and felt as if her lack of interest might contribute to that end.

The second reason she wanted to conclude the conversation quickly was that she had work to do.

A SECOND PLOT

As soon as Sarah hung up the phone with Raymond, she kicked into high gear. She remembered after our conversation the night before that the chiropractor didn't open his office until noon on Wednesdays and closed at five. She called him at home right after hanging up with Raymond and asked him a second time if he would be willing to help. He agreed and queried her for more information, but because of the time constraints, she only gave him the basic facts.

"I'll tell you more later on," she told him, "but I have to hurry now so I can get everything together for you to give to Raymond." She hung up with the doctor and began her tasks.

First, she wrote out a lone statement on a piece of paper that read as follows:

Raymond, I don't have the address where you and Daniel are staying. Could you please write it down on this piece of paper and give it to the doctor for me?

Then, on a second sheet of paper, she wrote out another message:

Raymond, do you want the police to come and rescue you from Daniel's control? If you do, call this number: (819) 579-7900 and tell the officer on duty.

Then below that, also on the second sheet of paper, she wrote another message:

For your information, Raymond, yesterday I took out a restraining order against Daniel. If he comes anywhere close to our house, or me, I can call the police and they will put him in jail. He will probably be served with that order tomorrow or Friday.

Below that, also on the second sheet of paper, Sarah listed several more scriptures for Raymond to look up. She finished the second sheet with:

Love, Sarah

After Sarah finished preparing her package for Raymond, she took a quick shower, dressed herself, and quickly fixed her hair. By then, it was nearly one in the afternoon. She hurried to the chiropractor's office, hoping she wasn't too late.

Fortunately, Sarah arrived before Raymond and Daniel, so she gave the doctor the two sheets of paper in a sealed envelope and offered him some quick instructions. She then zipped out the door and sped away from the building as quickly as possible to avoid meeting Raymond and Daniel.

Sarah's husband and his male lover didn't arrive until shortly after four that afternoon. The chiropractor saw them coming, so he turned up the music to cover any conversation he and Raymond may have in the adjustment room. When the two men came through the front door, the doctor played it like he had been an undercover cop his whole life.

He said from his office, "Hi, Raymond. I'll be right with you. Let me finish this paper I am working on."

Both Raymond and Daniel sat down in the waiting room. A few minutes later the doctor came out and stood before them.

With his intimidating six-foot six-inch, three-hundred-pound frame standing in front of them, he asked smiling, "Raymond, who is your friend?"

Raymond, very much under Daniel's control and secretly ashamed in front of everyone, said sheepishly, "Oh, this is Dan. He is working for me in my business."

The doctor reached out his hand to Daniel as Daniel stood up and said, "Good to meet you, Dan."

They shook hands as the chiropractor said, "This will only take a few minutes. Have a seat, Dan, and I'll have Raymond as good as new in no time."

The doctor motioned for Raymond to come into the back with him, and he closed the door. He then put his forefinger to his mouth to alert Raymond to silence and led him to the far corner of his adjustment room. Arriving there, he handed

Raymond Sarah's sealed envelope containing the two sheets of paper.

Raymond was ashamed, afraid, and nervous. Without commenting, he quickly and quietly opened the envelope and pulled out the contents. He read the first sheet he saw, grabbed a pen off the nearest table, wrote down his address, and gave it back to his doctor as the directions indicated. Though the music was louder than usual, Raymond felt reluctant to speak, apparently afraid that Daniel might hear.

Next, Raymond read the messages on the second sheet of paper. He revealed no facial expressions as he read about police involvement and the restraining order. He folded up the paper, tucked it into his pocket, offered the doctor a nod and a short, quiet "thank you," and hopped up onto the adjustment table.

Raymond said to his chiropractor, "Better do this quickly!"

The doctor was so surprised by Raymond's lack of conversation that he was uncomfortable speaking as well. The chiropractor was so afraid that he might say the wrong thing; he chose to say nothing. He simply went through his chiropractic routine, and then Raymond left.

The two men went out the front door, walked to Raymond's van, hopped in, and drove off leaving the doctor to wonder if he had squandered an opportunity to help his friend.

As soon as Raymond's vehicle was out of sight, the chiropractor called Sarah at home. She was not there so he read off the address onto the answer machine, let her know he had given the other paper to Raymond, and hung up.

Meanwhile, as soon as Raymond pulled out of the strip mall parking lot where the chiropractor's office was located, Daniel told Raymond to stop by Wendy's so he could grab a cheeseburger. He never mentioned a word about the chiropractor's office. It seemed that none of it aroused his suspicions. This was apparent when they parked in the Wendy's parking lot, because when Daniel exited the passenger side of the van, he didn't insist that Raymond come with him.

When Daniel said, "Let's go," Raymond responded, "Is it all right if I stay here? I need to relax my back after that workout."

To Raymond's surprise, Daniel didn't protest. He did, however, reach over, turn the vehicle off, and take the keys out of the ignition. Then he put them in his pocket and took them with him when he went into the restaurant, apparently figuring Raymond wouldn't leave without his van. Daniel did overlook one thing, though.

Just prior to going into the chiropractor's office, Daniel had tossed Raymond's cell phone onto the van's dash, apparently thinking it wouldn't be necessary inside. When they got back into the vehicle after leaving the chiropractor's office, Raymond noticed the phone was still there and that Daniel had not picked it up when they hopped into the truck. As Daniel walked through the parking lot toward Wendy's, Raymond almost desperately grabbed the phone and dialed Sarah at home. To his dismay, she wasn't home, but he left a message on the answer machine.

Raymond said frantically, "Sarah, what are you doing? You're going to mess everything up. As soon as Daniel is served with that restraining order, he is going to change his mind about letting me go with you back east in a few weeks. He is starting to get nervous about how I feel about you, so he made a deal with me to let me go with you. He said if he could go too, he would let me go as long as I wouldn't leave him. If you want me to go, you must stop that restraining order. I can't talk anymore. He's coming." Then Raymond hung up.

When Sarah arrived home, she listened to both messages and called me. She told me about the message the chiropractor left and Raymond's dispatch to her. I asked her how she felt about it.

She said, "Well, first, I had forgotten all about going back east. It was the furthest thing from my mind. We were supposed to go back there for a wedding in my family, but when all this mess started, I figured it was never going to happen anyway, so I forgot about it."

"But what about Raymond's reaction to the restraining order?" I asked. "How do you feel about that?"

"It sounds kind of weird—like Raymond isn't thinking right. The restraining order may help to free him from Daniel's control for good. But he is willing to stay under Daniel's power just for a trip to a wedding. It doesn't make sense. Daniel must have him so afraid that he can't think straight."

"Besides," she went on, "why would Raymond think that I would allow that creep to ride with us in a car several states away, anyway? I don't even want to see him again, let alone have him in our car for a four-day trip to and from my family's house, and for a week's vacation besides. Is Raymond crazy? If he was thinking correctly, he would be able to see that."

CONTROL

As I listened to Sarah on the phone, it all sounded confusing to me as well. It seemed more and more like Daniel's control over Raymond was very real.

How real?

Once the two men were a few weeks into their relationship, Daniel had his sights set on Raymond and all he could get from him. He saw him as a lover, a meal ticket, and a future; perhaps more of the latter, but all lacking in his life up until that point.

Never mind that Raymond had a house, a family, a business, a church, and a very involved life he had made for himself. Daniel saw and thought only of hope for himself. So, once he had his claws into Raymond, he wasn't going to let go.

Daniel would always prod Raymond, "Why don't you leave your wife and move in with me?"

These kinds of thoughts only seemed like playful suggestions until Daniel moved into his own place in the city where Raymond lived and did most of his business; but once in Raymond's town, Daniel's playful suggestions became much more serious.

Raymond had to admit, however, that he couldn't place all the blame on Daniel for the shift in Daniel's aggressiveness. Raymond had a significant personal interest in Daniel being closer in proximity as well.

Raymond thought if Daniel lived nearer to him, it would be much easier on him. Each day he had to drive a long way to pick Daniel up for work and then bring him back; and that was beginning to get expensive and time consuming. So, Raymond told Daniel it would really help him if he would consider moving into Raymond's city.

Raymond even said, "Listen, Daniel. I'll put up the money for your first month's rent. I'll put the apartment in my name, because your credit isn't good. I'll get you some furniture. We have some extra stuff—a bed, a dresser, and so forth. Christi has a couch and love seat that belonged to one of her friend's that you can use, and I'll buy you a television, so you won't be bored at night."

So, they did it. Daniel moved in the last week of August.

Once Daniel moved near Raymond, however, he became extremely possessive.

The time Raymond was supposed to pick Daniel up for work was seven in the morning, but if he showed up late, Daniel would throw a fit. He would berate Raymond mercilessly for not being on time. He would accuse Raymond of staying in bed too long with his wife and saddle him with a jealous and snotty employee for the first few hours of his day.

No sooner had Daniel moved into his new apartment, but he began to ask Raymond to spend the evenings with him. For a while Raymond put him off knowing Sarah's suspicions about their relationship may rise. But eventually, the pressure Daniel placed on him was too much and he began to give in.

Some nights, Raymond would eat dinner with Daniel at the apartment and then go home and eat another dinner with Sarah to hide his time spent with Daniel.

Finally, one night about a week before Day One, Raymond refused to stay the evening with Daniel, and Daniel responded, "If you don't stay with me until at least nine, I'll tell your wife about us."

The power play was off and running.

Then there was the business.

When Daniel and Raymond began their love and business relationship, Raymond agreed to pay his new employee ten dollars per hour. That would be enough to provide Daniel with adequate funds to support an apartment and meet his basic needs. As far as Daniel was concerned—at the beginning anyway—it was quite satisfactory.

Soon Daniel began doing most of the strenuous work, because he wanted to help and protect Raymond, because he was his lover. But just about the time he moved to Raymond's area, Daniel began to suggest to Raymond that his strenuous work deserved more pay.

He said, "I should receive at least twelve dollars an hour, because I am doing most of the work and all of the hard work."

Raymond told him he couldn't afford to pay him more because of his personal debt and high material costs. In time, however, Raymond bent under the pressure and conceded, "Maybe later, Daniel, when things begin to look up, and as I see my own finances begin to improve. Then, perhaps I can begin to pay you more an hour."

Daniel's response to Raymond was, "Fine, then. Until that happens, make me a fifty-fifty partner in your business as a good faith promise of your intentions."

Raymond wasn't willing to make him a partner, but Daniel kept nagging and pressuring him until, under duress, Raymond agreed halfheartedly. But Daniel claimed the weak verbal concession as a done deal.

During the last week before Sarah's Saturday night call to us, Daniel began pressuring Raymond nonstop to leave Sarah and live with him. Finally, the pleadings turned into manipulations.

Daniel said to Raymond, "I won't just tell Sarah about us. I will tell your pastor, your church, and all your customers about our relationship. I will ruin your reputation in this town, and neither of us will have a job."

There was, however, another issue.

Raymond had told Daniel that he and Sarah would be attending a wedding in Sarah's family out of state the last week in September. This event was eating at Daniel. It drove him crazy to think Raymond would be going away with Sarah and be with her in another state for an entire week while he would be alone in his apartment. The evil in Daniel was not about to let that happen. He wanted Raymond out of his house, away from Sarah, and solely under his control as soon as possible.

On the morning of the evening dinner party on Day One, Raymond told Daniel he couldn't come over to the apartment that night because he and Sarah were having guests for dinner.

Daniel's immediate and emphatic response was, "I'm coming to that dinner." It wasn't, "Can I come?" or, "Would I be able to come?" He said, "I will be there."

Because Raymond knew Sarah was becoming weary with his constant time spent with Daniel, he argued, "No! You can't come. I need to spend this time with my wife and our friends to help dispel her suspicions about us."

What Raymond didn't realize was that Daniel had no intention of playing second fiddle to Sarah. Nor did he intend that this love triangle he was in would have three sides for long. Daniel was going to put a stop to it, pronto! It seemed he had a clear and immediate deadline. He wanted to have Raymond all to himself before the dreaded wedding trip.

Daniel said to Raymond, "If you don't let me come to that dinner, I'll burst into your house and tell everyone about your relationship with me."

Raymond folded. Under the weight of Daniel's threats, Raymond agreed. Daniel was pulling the ultimate squeeze play on Raymond, and the pressure was getting greater than he could bear.

You will recall that in the middle of the evening dinner party on Day One, Raymond disrupted the event when he announced he needed to take Daniel home. Daniel had to be at the apartment to receive a regular call from his parole officer who was phoning to make sure he was home.

All the way to his apartment, Daniel laid into Raymond.

Daniel demanded, "You are telling your wife about us, and you are moving in with me tonight after your company leaves."

When they arrived at Daniel's apartment, he continued the harassment, saying once again, "If you don't tell Sarah tonight, I'll tell your pastor, your church, your friends, and your customers that you are gay, and I'll drag your reputation in this town through the mud. No one will ever hire you to build anything again."

All the playfulness in Daniel's suggestions about Raymond moving in with him was gone. For Daniel, it was all business now.

Raymond didn't know what to do other than comply. He was a powerless puppet.

Then, after the shocking announcement to Sarah, Daniel's oppression of Raymond hit overdrive. It did so largely because Daniel was feeling his own set of desperate issues.

Immediately following the announcement that Saturday night, he could see Raymond was feeling very uncertain. Raymond began to express his remorse about the decision, and Daniel could see it in Raymond's body language. Raymond told Daniel he didn't want to hurt his wife and daughter. Daniel noticed Raymond was uneasy and distant when he tried to talk to Raymond or touch him. It was all making Daniel nervous. He had too much at stake.

It wasn't just a love issue anymore. Daniel had stumbled onto a good thing, considering his current crisis, and he knew it. In his thinking he had landed a job, a business ownership, an apartment, a lover, and a future; and he wasn't going to let it slip out of his grasp. So, Daniel did the only thing he knew how to do. He took control.

The threats became more regular and more intense. Daniel started voicing them to Raymond with anger and gritted teeth. They weren't lightly stated as possibilities anymore. They were now genuine threats, and they intensified consistently from the beginning of Day One until around Day Three. At this point, Daniel began to realize that the potency of his threats had diminished, because most of the people he threatened to tell about his and Raymond's relationship already knew. That is when Daniel began to threaten harm.

He began with himself. He started by saying to Raymond, "If you leave me to go back with Sarah, I'll commit suicide. I'll take my own life, because without you, Raymond, I won't be able to live."

After a while, he abandoned his suicide threats, because he sensed his control tactics weren't compatible with threats to take his own life. Control was powerful, while suicide was powerless, and therefore not believable. It wouldn't be long before Raymond would cease to believe that Daniel would really go through with killing himself.

At that point Daniel started to threaten harm to others, not directly or obviously, but subtly at first. He did this because he knew exact threats would be construed as a parole violation.

He would say things like, "If you leave me, Raymond, it won't be good for Sarah and Christi. You may think it will, but trust me, they will pay a huge price, and so will you, Raymond, if you leave me."

By Wednesday, however, Daniel's mask over his threats had become quite thin, and the intent of his words very clear.

He started saying to Raymond with little restraint, "If you don't stay with me, I will hurt anyone and everyone who is close to you, Sarah, Christi, your friends, and your pastor. I will make you so sorry you ever left me that you will suffer the rest of your life for what you did to me."

By this time, Raymond's equilibrium was so mentally and emotionally out of sorts that he was not thinking rationally. Daniel had oppressed him with so much fear for his own safety and the safety of people he cared about, Raymond was in no condition to make logical choices. He merely moved, thought, and reacted like the puppet Daniel had made of him.

LACK OF POLICE FORCE

As I listened to Sarah talk, I could tell it was as clear to her as it was to me, that Raymond's thought processes were not reasonable, no doubt a by-product of Daniel's sway over him.

Both of us felt that without the restraining order there was little else we knew to do. The restraining order was the only connection we had with the police, and we were feeling more and more that the kind of danger that surrounded the situation could very well mandate police intervention at some point. We didn't want to stop the only legal order that kept the police connected to our crisis. It was Sarah's decision to *not* stop the restraining order regardless of Raymond's reaction to it.

Unbeknownst to us, while we were talking on the phone that evening, Raymond received a call from the police officer Sarah had talked to on Tuesday. When the phone rang, Daniel answered it.

The officer calling identified himself and asked for Raymond. As usual, Daniel leaned his ear into the receiver to eavesdrop. The officer simply asked Raymond if he was all right.

"Yes," responded Raymond, fearing what Daniel might do should he say no.

The officer said, "Your wife called and thought someone might be holding you against your will. Are you being held by force?"

Raymond answered, "No, of course not," as Daniel glared at him.

"Are you able to answer of your own free choice or is someone influencing you to speak against your will?" the officer asked.

Raymond said with Daniel monitoring every word the two men were saying, "I am speaking entirely for myself with no one influencing me."

The officer said, "Well, OK then. I just wanted to be sure you were all right. You'll give us a call if you need us, won't you?"

Raymond answered, "Yes, I will."

When they hung up, Daniel said, "That wife of yours isn't very smart. She had better watch herself or she might wind up in deep trouble, and it will be your fault, Raymond."

MOTHER-DAUGHTER TALK # 3

After Sarah finished telling me about the events of the day, I prayed with her and said good-bye for the evening.

That night when Christina came home, Sarah met her at the front door, took her by the hand, and brought her into the living room.

After sitting her down, she said, "Christi, I know you have said you are not afraid of Daniel, but we think your dad is very afraid of him. When I told him about the restraining order, he asked me to stop it, but I am not going to, because I feel we need to do everything we can to get Daniel away from Daddy. With the restraining order, if Daniel comes anywhere close to me or our house, he violates his parole, and they will take him and put him in jail—no questions asked."

Christi said, "If that is what you feel you need to do, fine. But I am not going to change the way I live because of Daniel."

They talked for a little while longer, and then both went to bed.

However, Sarah went to sleep with mixed feelings. She felt great apprehension concerning Raymond. She still didn't know where her relationship with him would end up. These thoughts caused her so much discomfort that she chose to shed them almost as soon as they surfaced. She also felt very fearful for Raymond's safety.

While she thought fearful thoughts about Raymond, she was feeling good thoughts about Christina. She felt like the hard-distant heart she had observed in her daughter over the last year had taken a softer turn over the last few days. It was a touch of joy she was feeling amid great trepidation. She found herself holding onto the promise in Psalm 91:15–16 for both her husband and Christina.

It says:

"He shall call upon Me, and I will answer him; I will be with him in trouble; I will deliver him and honor him. With long life I will satisfy him and show him My salvation."

As Sarah thought on these things, she fell fast asleep, and for the first time in five days, slept soundly.

That was Day Five.

DAY SIX
THURSDAY

I rose early on Thursday morning and made a beeline for the church to study. I could foresee the Gil crisis lingering on indefinitely, though I was hoping for an imminent resolve. I felt the urgency to get things done while I had the opportunity. I didn't call Sarah and hoped she wouldn't call me until I had made more progress on the work I had to finish up. God was good to me though. The thoughts flowed and interruptions were minimal, so I was able to make significant headway on my sermon, excepting finishing touches by about one thirty that afternoon.

Feeling as if a huge load had been lifted, and more prepared for whatever the Gil emergency might unfold, I called Sarah to find out the latest. When she answered the phone, however, she was noticeably upset, and I sensed the adrenaline level within me on the rise.

"What's wrong, Sarah?" I asked, feeling her anxiousness even through the phone lines.

She said, "I received a call from Raymond earlier this morning, and I can tell he is just not right. It is all the same things we were saying yesterday. But now I'm almost certain that Daniel is threatening to hurt Raymond or me or Christi or maybe all of us if Raymond doesn't do what he wants."

I should have been prepared for the tension in the crisis to still be high, but I wasn't. That let me know the stress of the issue at hand, even for me, was significant as well. It would have been a pleasant relief to my ears to hear Sarah say a miracle took place overnight, such as: Raymond came home for good, or Daniel left for greener pastures, or better yet was back in jail. The grief I felt that no miracles had materialized since the night before was an unwelcomed shock back into reality for me.

"Well," I said, hoping my disappointment was not detectable in my voice, "what did Raymond say?"

"It wasn't really what he said as much as it was what he didn't say," she answered as if she were still analyzing his words to her that morning. She continued, "I just decided I was going to quit playing around and not worry about whether Daniel was listening. I decided if Raymond called, I would just ask him straight out. So, I did."

"And what happened?" I insisted, showing my impatience.

"Well, I just asked him, 'Do you want to stay with Daniel or not?' And Raymond responded in a tone that let me know without a doubt that he was definitely trying to hide something from me or Daniel."

"What did he say?" I asked, revealing my rapidly rising concern.

She said, "He responded, 'Well…not exactly. But that's just the way it has to be right now.'"

Sarah went on, "Then I asked him, 'Is Daniel threatening to hurt you, Raymond?' But Daniel must have been looking at him or getting his sleazy ear up next to the phone to hear, because Raymond just changed the subject. He answered me with something random like, 'Isn't it a nice day?' or something like that. Then he said, 'Well, Daniel and I have to go to work. If I need something, I'll call you.'"

"That Daniel makes me so mad," Sarah continued. "He must have Raymond too scared to say anything. But I don't know what to do. What do you think?" she asked me in a desperate voice. "How do you feel about it? What do you think about what Raymond said on the answer machine on Monday?"

Now, I remembered Sarah referring to that message, but she only said it concerned her. I didn't remember her telling me Raymond's precise words, and she hadn't referred to it again until that moment.

I said, "Sarah, I remember you telling me about that, but I don't recall whether or not you told me exactly what Raymond said. Tell me again. What did Raymond actually say?"

"Would you like to hear it? I didn't erase it from the answer machine, so I still have it."

Surprised, I asked, "You still have it?" Then I said emphatically, "Yes, by all means play it for me."

So, Sarah played the whole message back to me over the phone. It was a little fuzzy, but easy enough to understand; and I could tell without question it was Raymond's voice. The first part of the message was a hurried explanation about Daniel controlling Raymond's phone and monitoring his calls. But his last words before he hung up were frightening. Confirming all of our suspicions, Raymond said with terror in his voice, "I just don't know what to do. He's threatening me and my family."

Those words pushed me over the edge. The urgency factor in my heart concerning the matter instantly rose beyond my ability to hold back my emotions.

I said with what must have seemed like anger at her, "Sarah, why didn't you let me hear that message before this? That is an extremely significant statement."

I was angry, but not at Sarah. I was angry at the devil, at Daniel, at the police department, and maybe at myself for not getting fired up sooner.

Then Sarah said, "There's something else I didn't tell you. Yesterday I got a call from Raymond. When I answered, I could hear Raymond and Daniel talking in the background. It seemed like he had pressed the call button, but I couldn't tell if he had done it by accident or on purpose, so I just listened. I listened for a long time. They were arguing about the business for much of the time, and two times during their discussion, Daniel shouted at Raymond, 'If you don't do what I tell you, I'll bash your head in.' But when he said it, he wasn't saying it like it was just something to say. He screamed it at Raymond like he was out of control. It really scared me."

I broke in, "Sarah, that was what I needed to hear. I am going to call the police department, but this time I am going to make sure they start taking us seriously."

POLICE AGAIN

I hung up with Sarah and wasted no time calling the police.

A receptionist answered the phone. Before she had a chance to say any more than her greeting, I began to unload all the stress that had built up inside me over the last five days.

"Ma'am," I said, "My name is Chris Schimel. I am the pastor of a church here in town, and I have an extremely dangerous situation I am dealing with concerning a family in our church. We are in desperate need of help from the police department, and we can't seem to get them to take any interest. We called on Monday and talked to an officer in training, but he never returned our call."

I gave her no room to insert a response. I just went on with my volume increasing as I went.

"We talked to someone else on Tuesday," I said, "and we told him we felt a person in our church was being intimidated and held against his will. He said the police couldn't do anything to help unless we get permission from that person, and we can't do that, because he is being kept from us. Do you understand what I am telling you?"

By this time, I was almost shouting at the poor lady, but I didn't come to a halt.

"We took out a restraining order against the person causing the problem, but people could be dead before the order is served. We need some help, and we need it now, and I am not hanging up until you tell me that there is something you are going to do to help us."

I almost shocked myself talking so boldly to people who could legally thump me like a bug. I expected a rebuke for my candidness or something worse.

Apparently, however, the receptionist was not offended at my aggression. Instead, she calmed me down skillfully and professionally. Then she asked me to provide her with enough details so she could analyze our situation more effectively.

After I took a few minutes to fill in the blanks, she responded, "Yes, I believe there is something that can be done. I think we can do a welfare check. I am going to give this to Officer Jay Seaver. He is in a briefing right now, but I believe he will be done in about forty-five minutes. I will have him call you as soon as he is finished."

I hung up somewhat more encouraged than when I picked up the receiver. At least I had heard someone say they could assist us. But here I was, waiting for a return call from the police again.

By now I was so skeptical of their ability or desire to take action, I almost had myself convinced that when I would finally talk to the officer, some detail or loophole would cause him to conclude as the other two officers had, that they couldn't get involved either. I even doubted if the officer would call me back.

So, as I waited, I strategized. *If we were to secure about three large men from our church, go over to Raymond's and Daniel's apartment, separate the two men, and do the talking, maybe some police officers would at least stand by and protect us. Perhaps our taking that kind of action would coax the police department to get involved.*

To my surprise, in forty-five minutes Officer Seaver did call back.

By then I had calmed down considerably and took about ten minutes to tell him the story of the last six days. When I finished, I shared with him my idea about the three large men from our church. He said he thought it was a good idea and commendable for us to want to help, but he couldn't allow us to do it, because it was too dangerous.

I almost let out a shout right there on the phone. Someone from the police department agreed with us. The situation *was* serious. It didn't take long for me to realize that this officer was experienced, but more importantly, he was genuinely concerned. He spent several minutes with me discussing our options.

THE PLAN

This is the plan we came up with: first, Officer Jay needed to secure permission from Sarah to perform a welfare check on Raymond.

A welfare check was a visit from the police to someone reported to them to be under duress of some kind. The visit is designed to be an intervention, if there is a problem. On the other hand, if there are no difficulties occurring, that fact will be discovered instead.

The officer said he didn't need Raymond's permission to do this; he only needed Sarah's. He assured me he would call her as soon as we finished talking to acquire her approval as well as obtain Raymond's and Daniel's address. He also wanted to hear Raymond's taped message from Monday for himself.

Second, he and another officer would pay a visit to Daniel and Raymond between nine and nine thirty that night. Officer Seaver would take Raymond to the side, where he would be away from Daniel's influence, and ask him if he wanted to stay or leave. The other officer would stay with Daniel to prevent him from getting near Raymond. If Raymond chose to stay, their task would be over. If he chose to leave, it would be, as we expected, that Raymond was being pressured to stay against his will.

But there was another issue, and that was safety.

None of us, including Officer Seaver, were convinced that if Raymond were to leave, Daniel would compliantly roll over and let his plan to make a life for himself just die. He may react the way disturbed people do when they can't have what they want. He may devise another plan or want to hurt Raymond or Sarah or Christina—maybe all of them. He may even want to hurt Shirley and me. The officer's concern was that if Daniel was as irrational as he seemed from the information we had given him, there was no telling how he might react. Daniel may say, "If I can't have Raymond, no one can, and everyone hindering us from being together is going to pay."

So, we decided to make sure none of us were home or in a place where Daniel might be able to find us. My wife and I would pick up Sarah and have her with us at my office in the church from eight thirty to ten that night. That location was a little risky since the Gils spent a lot of time there. But we decided to use it because it would be an easy place for Raymond to find. We would also talk to Christina and have her come to the church as well for her safety. If she chose not to come there, we wanted to be sure she wasn't at home or at a place where Daniel could find her.

The most important part of the safety plan was that Officer Seaver would tell Raymond his family was in a safe location so he could feel free to leave, knowing his wife and daughter were out of danger. If Raymond chose to leave, Officer Jay would also tell him where we were so he could go there as well.

Furthermore, I asked the officer if he thought we should put up the whole Gil family in an out-of-town hotel overnight in case Daniel might be thinking about immediate revenge. That way Daniel wouldn't be able to find them to hurt them.

Together, we decided if Raymond indeed left Daniel and came to the church, it would probably be a good thing to consider.

Another issue we discussed was Daniel's parole. Both officers would try to secure information from either of the men concerning the level of threats Daniel was imposing on Raymond. If Raymond or Daniel revealed or directly reported a threat given to Raymond suggesting harm to him or anyone else, they would slap the cuffs on Daniel right then and there.

Somewhere in my conversation with Officer Seaver I learned he was a Christian and went to a church I was familiar with. That gave me great peace because it suggested his concern for our situation wasn't only connected to his code of ethics as a police officer to protect and serve; it was also tied to his walk with Christ. He was answering to a higher authority than just the city he served. He was answering to God.

At last, I thought, with a great sense of relief, *we've found someone in an official place of influence who truly cares.*

After hanging up with Officer Seaver, I gave him time to reach Sarah before I called her. When I did, I was pleased to hear from her that the policeman had already called, and she was greatly encouraged with his concern as well. She told me that when he called, he asked if he could hear the taped message from Raymond, and she told him of Daniel's words about bashing Raymond's head in. The officer was also noticeably alarmed. I talked with Sarah about the plans Officer Seaver and I had discussed, and she was in full agreement.

Surrounding this whole ordeal was Sarah's full compliance. At no time did she try to devise her own plans. She trusted Shirley's and my leadership throughout. She ran everything by us. If she had an idea or opinion, she would always talk to us before she acted. And if we felt her idea was not the best, she would abandon it quickly and compliantly. It greatly increased the weight of responsibility I felt in the crisis, but I knew we were the ones to oversee it and follow it through to its conclusion.

Our church was small. We had a few staff personnel, but none had the freedom in their schedules to spend time advising and attending to Sarah as we did. Furthermore, by this time, only a few people in our church knew about the crisis, and the nature of the ordeal seemed to beg for that anonymity to remain.

I had talked with our elders about the Gil situation at our leadership meeting the Sunday before. They were praying for the Gils, and I had talked with a few of them during the week to keep them informed and to stay accountable. But we were the elected ones to handle this tumultuous trial, and I was very aware of the seriousness involved. I also felt the weight of the dependency Sarah had placed upon us. It was a precarious position to be in indeed, but it was apparent that God wanted us to be there nonetheless.

After I prayed with Sarah concerning the success of the welfare check, I hung up and called my wife to tell her about the plan we devised with Officer Seaver.

We didn't have time to catch our breath that night. I had to remain at church as long as I could to get some more work finished, though my concentration on the tasks I needed to complete was not very focused.

There were way too many wandering thoughts—thoughts of what might happen and what I would do if they did— thoughts about possible dangers for me and my wife—thoughts about possible funerals, wakes, eulogies, and so forth. Maybe all my fears were extreme, but they were no doubt representative of the stress I was feeling at the time.

There was a lot of prayer going up from us as well as from our church leadership and the few Christians that Sarah had contacted by then. We made many of our decisions standing on Psalm 37:23: *"The steps of a good man are ordered by the Lord, And He delights in his way."*

There wasn't time to have a prayer meeting with Sarah. There wasn't opportunity to call the leadership together to have them intercede over us or seek their advice, though I did run a few things by some of them during that week. Sarah was praying; her friends were praying; our church leadership was praying; and Shirley and I were praying. Mostly, however, many of my prayers were being sent heavenward while I was on the run. We were making rapid fire decisions and counting on all the prayer being offered to act as a covering for us.

The way I saw it, Raymond, Sarah, Christi, and even Shirley and myself had entered harm's way through this ordeal. Without question, my wife and I were the least likely candidates for Daniel's wrath, but I felt we shouldn't eliminate ourselves from the potential victim's list—at least not yet. Officer Seaver cautioned me that we were all possible targets, so Shirley and I should be cautious as well.

Raymond, Sarah, and Christi were in the greatest danger. With Raymond, the concerns were obvious, but Christi and Sarah both had their run-ins with Daniel that week, and it heightened the scope of concern for all three of them.

After Sarah finished talking with me, she called Christina on her cell to tell her about our plans and the welfare check to take place that evening. As we suspected, Christina didn't want to wait with her mom, Shirley and me at the church. She did agree, however, not to go home; though she never flinched in her bid to not fear Daniel. She did agree; her dad knowing she was in a safe place might be beneficial in helping him to leave Daniel, so she conceded.

When she finished work at six that night, she would hook up with some of her friends and hang out for the rest of the evening without going home. But she would leave her cell phone on so Sarah could keep her informed throughout the evening.

Christina worked as a cashier at a local clothing store in our city. Daniel knew where she worked, but since her shift ended around dinnertime that night, she wouldn't be in a location where Daniel could find her at the time of the welfare check.

After my call to my wife, I tried to get a few more things finished with the evening's forthcoming confrontation looming on my mind. I made a quick call to my elders to inform them of the plan for that evening and they all said they would be in prayer from nine to nine thirty.

When I had no more time to simultaneously work and worry, I scampered home in time to gulp down a few bites, round up my wife, and dash back to the Gils's house to pick up Sarah.

WELFARE CHECK

We picked Sarah up at exactly eight thirty and went over to the church. We parked our car where Raymond could see it and left the front door unlatched so he could enter without difficulty. But we left my office door, where we waited, locked for our safety. We talked and watched the clock out of the corners of our eyes.

Sarah was pretty good at conversation, anyway, but she was especially talkative as we waited that night. I knew it reflected the nervousness in her heart.

As we sat there, with Sarah chattering anxiously, I thought, *how did we get here?* Never in the ministry had I found myself in a crisis such as this.

I also wondered as I sat waiting and listening to Sarah's jittery prattles...*what must be going on in her heart about wanting her husband back?*

I remembered what she said about that subject earlier that week after she had received the unsolicited suggestions from her friends. But it was a few days later now, and Raymond was perhaps very close to coming home. Did she still feel the same? Was she considering trying to make a go of her marriage after this was over?

I knew in Christ, there was great power to forgive and find reconciliation, but this scenario was unlike anything

I had ever encountered before. Was her tenacity to stick by Raymond and acquire him back a "love is forever" type of thing, or was it merely competition? Was she going to try and win in this power struggle with Daniel, and then when it was over, find that no love remained in her heart for Raymond? Instinctively, I knew she would have ample support for that strain of thinking. By this time, she was already receiving plenty of encouragement from people to abandon her husband for what he had done to her.

Another splinter in my mind had to do strictly with Raymond. *Once we got him back and safe—then what?* Would he be like a vagabond or outcast without a friend, without a job, without a wife, and without a family? I knew the church and I would have to take him in. God wouldn't allow me to reject him. Nor would He allow me to encourage the church to cast him aside. But would Raymond be able to handle all the self-imposed self-esteem challenges his sin and guilt would place on him?

Over the years, I've seen people in the church go through things such as divorce, affairs, or various other kinds of indiscretions. With many, it didn't matter how much I loved them, or the church accepted them, their shame alone caused them to see rejection that wasn't even there. As a result, they would leave the church; or their relationship with the Lord, or their family, just because of their inability to deal with their own inner condemnation. My perception as I sat there in my office that night listening to Sarah talk was simple: Raymond's mess made other people's messes, no matter how severe, look like a walk in the park. I feared, *what would happen to Raymond?*

Then there was Daniel. Were we going to be rid of him? Would he be carted off to jail or would he hang around to be a thorn in all our sides? I was concerned about his soul, but my much experience with people told me there was one chance in a million he could hang around, be converted, and coexist with Sarah and Raymond in the same state, let alone the same city.

My concentration broke when Sarah began to cry, and my wife moved next to her to be a comfort. I moved out of my seat and found a place in front of her as well, kneeling on the floor. It was clear that the stress of the week was getting to her right about then. Frankly, it was getting to all of us. Shirley, from beside Sarah on the couch, hugged her. I took her hand and we both consoled her.

In response to our comfort, she apologized, collected herself: and we returned to our seats to continue to listen to Sarah's much-needed therapy session. I looked at the clock. It was nine thirty-five and still no word...and no Raymond.

Meanwhile, at about the same time, Officer Seaver and his partner went to Raymond and Daniel's door. When they knocked, Daniel answered.

Officer Jay asked, "Is Raymond Gil here?"

With a smile on his face, Daniel responded, "Sure, he's right here." Then he turned to Raymond who was sitting on the couch and said, "Raymond, there are a couple of police officers here who would like to speak with you."

When Raymond came to the door, Officer Jay asked him, "Are you Raymond Gil?"

"Yes," answered Raymond apprehensively.

Officer Jay posed a second question, "Sir, can I talk to you alone outside here?" Raymond looked at Daniel as if to obtain permission.

"You don't need my permission," Daniel said with a casual smile on his face. "You're a grown man," he followed, then looked at the officers shaking his head and laughing as if to suggest, "There's no forced captivity going on here." But they all knew there was. The officers knew there was. Raymond knew there was. Daniel knew there was. And Daniel knew that everyone else knew there was. But everyone played the game of not knowing.

Raymond moved quickly out the door and over to the side of the front yard with Officer Jay, about thirty feet away from the sidewalk that led to their apartment.

Officer Jay said, "Raymond, before I talk to you about what I came here for, I want to let you know something. Your pastor, Chris, and his wife Shirley, have Sarah with them at the church. She is not home. She is safe with the Schimels and Christina is not home either. She is out with friends, and there is no way Daniel could hurt anyone in your family. They are all safe."

Raymond listened intently, carefully analyzing the picture Officer Jay was painting for him.

Officer Jay asked him, "Do you understand what I am telling you?"

Raymond didn't answer; he merely shook his head yes as he stretched his neck to look over the cop's shoulder to see where Daniel was.

Officer Seaver then said, "Raymond, I talked to your wife today after your pastor called me. They asked me if I would come and see if you are OK. They are concerned that Daniel is keeping you here against your will with threats against you or your family. Raymond, has Daniel threatened any kind of physical harm to you or anyone close to you?"

Raymond again stretched his neck slightly and stood up on his tiptoes enough to raise his eyesight over the officer's shoulder to see if Daniel was still inside. Daniel and Officer Seaver's partner were standing in the doorway. The other officer was distracting Daniel with conversation.

Raymond, who seemed to be hemming and hawing, answered the policeman, "Well . . . he hasn't actually threatened us with physical harm . . . no . . . he has never actually threatened to hurt any of us physically."

Officer Jay looked at Raymond suspiciously, took a deep breath, and asked, "Well then, is this man holding you against your will?"

Again, Raymond answered nervously, as if he weren't practicing full disclosure, "Well . . . uh . . . no, I guess I could leave if I wanted."

Officer Seaver was quite confused. Raymond's body language told a story of fear. But his words spoke otherwise.

"All right then, Raymond," said Officer Seaver. "Since your family is safe, do you want to leave?"

Raymond looked up at the policeman who stood at least ten inches taller than him and asked somewhat pathetically, "Can I?"

Officer Jay said, "You may. Just go inside, pack some things as quickly as you can, and leave."

"Chris, Shirley, and Sarah are at the church?"

"They are!"

Raymond looked over at Daniel, then back at the policeman standing in front of him. He then broke for the door past the other officer and Daniel without looking either of them in the eye. He threw some things into a bag as quickly as he could, grabbed his keys and phone, and ran out the door toward his van. He scurried around the front of his vehicle as fast as his short little legs would carry him, hopped in, started the engine, and squealed out of the parking lot.

Officer Seaver watched curiously as Raymond took full advantage of his opportunity to escape his current situation.

Officer Seaver reasoned; *Raymond's statements and his actions didn't line up. If there were no threats and no forced captivity, then why was Raymond so anxious to leave, and why would he ask the officer's permission to do so?* He concluded that it was all related to the fear Raymond must have been feeling with Daniel.

After Raymond was gone, the officer focused his attention on Daniel. He walked over to the front door and asked the parolee directly, "Daniel, have you been threatening to harm Raymond or his family or anyone they know in any way?"

Daniel responded with a surprised look and tone, "No, absolutely not. Why? Did Raymond tell you that?"

Officer Jay looked hard into Daniel's eyes as Daniel looked equally hard back into his and said, "It hasn't been served, yet, but it will be. Mrs. Gil has taken out a restraining order against you. So, if I were you, I would stay away from this family from this point on. I know you are on parole, and if you are caught violating that order, you will be back in prison to stay for a long time."

Daniel said innocently, "Hey! I don't want any trouble. Raymond was here because he wanted to be. He could have left any time he wanted. He knew that."

AT CHURCH

It was quarter to ten when Raymond showed up. He appeared it seemed, out of thin air. I heard a slight knock on the door, rose to open it, and he slipped through the opening and slid sheepishly onto the couch beside Sarah. Instantly, he formed himself into a ball on the couch with his hands folded together between his legs, which were both squeezed tightly together. He was bent over at the shoulders and his head hung almost down into his lap as if he were ashamed, overcome with guilt, and terrified all at the same time. He didn't say a word. He just sat there beside his wife in a fetal position, folded over, rocking slightly forward and backward.

Sarah, Shirley, and I all rushed to him and hugged him simultaneously, embracing whatever part of his upper body that was exposed.

"Raymond, are you all right? How do you feel? Are you hurt?" we asked in chorus. Raymond didn't answer; he just began to whimper and sniffled as if he was a tear-filled four-year-old calming down after screams of terror from a skinned knee.

We held him until Raymond seemed to lightly shed our embrace, not as a rejection, but as if he didn't deserve it. Sarah continued to sit beside him with her arm around his shoulder, holding him tightly. He held his fetal pose though, apparently still feeling ashamed and afraid.

Then he began to thank us.

Crying, sobbing, and still with his head down, Raymond said over and over repetitively and with obvious sincerity, "Thank you so much for saving me. Thank you. Thank you. You saved my life. Thank you for what you did. I don't know if I can ever repay you. Thank you. Thank you. Thank you," he went on.

As if the same instinct settled on all three of us at once, we knew together not to ask Raymond anymore questions until he had collected himself. So, we all just sat there, Sarah by his side, still hugging his shoulders, and Shirley and I in our seats leaning forward with our gaze on Raymond until he quit whimpering.

As we sat there, my mind explored the terror Raymond must have gone through over the prior six days.

Raymond was somewhat stocky, though short; and he was a gruff man. In our church his very demeanor struck fear in many people's hearts. His deep, guttural voice and often stiff, impenetrable posture had some church members comparing him to Genghis Kahn. Yet, as I sat there in contemplation, I could see that all of his previous intimidations toward people seemed not believable, as I observed what appeared to be terror in him unlike I had seen in anyone before. I had no information from his lips to tell me this; I just knew.

Finally, Raymond began to speak. He didn't share any information to shed light on the previous week's events. He just began to utter laments.

"I'm so ashamed," Raymond said, still with his head hanging low. "I feel so embarrassed for what I've done. I knew it was wrong, but I did it anyway, and I don't know why. Sarah, how can you ever forgive me? I'll understand if you don't. If you want me to move out, I'll understand. Chris, how can I ever look you in the face again? If you want me to leave the church, I will. No one in church will forgive me, and I don't blame them. I know what I've done is wrong. I have ruined my family. Christina probably won't have any respect for me at all. My customers won't have any use for me anymore after Daniel gets done telling them about me. I've ruined my life."

Then he started to cry again.

It wasn't as if we were set to scold him, but he seemed to feel sure it was what he deserved. Who, at that moment, could have added to the punishment Raymond was already imposing on himself by offering a rebuke?

As his self-condemnation subsided, I said, "Raymond, we don't feel any of that. We are just glad you are safe."

I felt bad for Raymond and the shame he must have been going through. But I was still very focused on the task of eliminating a danger source. Though Raymond was sitting in my office, seemingly safe after the near weeklong ordeal, I wasn't convinced Daniel was completely out of the picture.

I went on, "Raymond, I know you are upset, but could you tell me...did Daniel threaten to harm you or your family? Did he say he would hurt, or maybe even kill, somebody close to you?"

I was hoping Raymond would confirm what we suspected—that Daniel had indeed uttered to Raymond a threat upon his family. In fact, I was sure Raymond would confirm so. I felt like the best place for Daniel, and the safest for the Gils, was for the convict to be back in prison to stay.

But Raymond would not betray Daniel. I couldn't tell if his protection of Daniel was from a fear of reprisal, blind love for the criminal, or honesty from Raymond.

Raymond responded, a bit more engaged with us, but not in convincing tones, "No . . . uh . . . Daniel never really said he would . . . uh . . . hurt me or my family. He said he would hurt himself. He said he would ruin my reputation . . . and . . . that I would be . . . be . . . sorry if I ever left him. But he never really said he would physically harm any of us."

Without having the benefit of Officer Seaver's account of his talk with Raymond at the apartment, I was feeling my own confusion with Raymond's protection of Daniel. It didn't make sense that Raymond would sob in mortal terror, thanking us repeatedly for saving his life, and then say there was really no threat of harm going on.

"Raymond," I said, "what about what Sarah heard Daniel say about bashing your head in? And what about the message you left on your answer machine Monday from the dentist's office? On that message, you clearly said that Daniel was threatening you and your family. That sounds like a threat to me."

Raymond answered thoughtfully, but still not convincingly. "Well . . . he did say he would hurt us . . . but my impression was . . . uh . . . he meant he would hurt our family's reputation in our city and in church . . . and he would . . . hurt my business. He always said he would bash my head in. It's just an expression he uses."

I was thoroughly frustrated. I felt strongly Daniel was still a major concern and was looking for any small excuse to have him put away, but no opportunities were availing themselves. I also suspected, with Daniel's previous experiences in prison with other convicts and the justice system, he probably did have a fair read on what to say and what not to say that might bring trouble his way. Surely Daniel knew an outright threat of physical harm against someone would violate his parole and put him behind bars again. He must know that if he were going to make threats of any kind, he would need to dance carefully around the precise threat of physical harm. But Raymond's perspective had me baffled.

I said, "All right, Raymond. It sounds like Daniel was at least smart enough to choose the right words to say, but in all of his threats, were you at any time afraid for your own, or your family's physical well-being?"

Raymond looked up and stared at me thoughtfully for what seemed like an eternity and said, "Uh . . . yeah . . . I guess so."

Well, it was an admission . . . sort of. But there was certainly nothing there that could be called criminal on Daniel's part. What bothered me most was that I wasn't sure Raymond was disclosing everything in his heart.

Just about then there was a loud knock at the entrance door of our church. After Raymond had slipped in and sat down on my couch, and while he was sniffling, I had gone out to close and lock the door in case Daniel might suspect our whereabouts and decide to pay us a visit. So, I approached the foyer carefully. I was surprised, however, to see a police officer standing at our church's front door. I opened it and Officer Jay Seaver introduced himself to me.

Officer Seaver was a tall man, perhaps six feet four inches in height. He appeared healthy and strong and talked with a deep, resonate voice, seemingly by divine design to intimidate any would-be lawbreakers.

I invited him in and began to question him right there by the door. His answers provided me a description of the welfare check from beginning to end. We stood there exchanging this information for at least ten minutes. He shared with me his confusion about Raymond's fear and anxious willingness to leave in contrast to his unwillingness to tie Daniel to any serious threats. But his next words chilled me to the bone.

He said, "After Raymond ran to his van and drove off, I talked real straight to Mr. Rogers. I told him that he better leave this family alone or he was going to find himself back in jail in a hurry. But when I looked into his eyes, I saw something I had never seen before in all my years as a cop." He said with almost terror in his voice, "I saw evil...pure evil. I've seen evil things and evil people before. But I have never looked into a person's eyes and seen evil itself. But that's what I saw when I looked at Daniel Rogers."

I didn't know what to say. He stood there for the longest time looking at me, waiting for a reaction. And I stood looking at him for just as long with my mouth open and feeling my heart forcing itself up my throat.

Finally, leaving his last thought as if he were afraid to pursue it further, he asked, "So, is Raymond here?"

"Yes," I answered, though I was having a bit more difficulty refocusing my mind to a new thought. "He's in my office."

"Maybe we had better go in and talk to him," said the policeman.

I checked the door to be sure it was tightly locked and directed Officer Jay through the doors, leading to where my wife, Sarah, and Raymond were sitting. He and I sat down, and the officer immediately took the floor.

He said, "Raymond, are you all right?"

Raymond responded, "Yes. Thank you so much for helping me. Thank you so much."

By then, we all knew we had averted a very real disaster, though Raymond was less forthcoming with his admission about it. We talked with the large policeman for several minutes. Officer Jay was not at peace that the threat called *Daniel Rogers* was over.

We decided the Gils, including Christina, should not spend the night at home. However, since Raymond had put so much money into Daniel, his finances were running on empty. I told them the church would pay for the three of them to stay overnight in a hotel nearby in case Daniel was looking for payback.

Officer Jay agreed. He was convinced Daniel's motivation, should he attempt reprisal, would be connected to the loss of a meal ticket. He saw Raymond as a hope for a new life, and along with that came great satisfaction that he had landed such a fortuitous opportunity. Then, just like that, it all went sour and did so in a whirl of rejection from Raymond. The officer felt that could easily ignite a fuse of revenge in the heart of someone as angry and as evil as he had discerned Daniel to be.

"Yes," said Officer Jay, "I think it would be wise that no one in the Gil family stay at home tonight."

So, I called the hotel and made the arrangements.

The lawman also instructed Raymond and Sarah to go to the police department first thing in the morning and have his name and Christina's put on the restraining order before they would have it served to Daniel. He also told Raymond to have myself and Shirley, our home, the church, and any business customer or jobsite where he would work in the next few weeks, put on the order as well.

As I listened to Jay Seaver, I felt ashamed I had demonstrated negative emotions toward the Police Department. Officer Jay was obviously very engaged and thorough in his concern for the Gils and the whole situation. As the policeman spoke, I was beginning to feel a sense of security for them—like a high and impenetrable wall of iron was being erected about them.

HOTEL

We decided Christina shouldn't meet her mom and dad at home. Instead she should rendezvous with them at a neutral location, park one of the automobiles there, and drive in one vehicle to the hotel. In the morning they could all leave the hotel early and return home to prepare for the day. Raymond called his daughter and told her of the plans we had formulated. He arranged to meet her at a neutral parking lot where they could connect and get to their accommodations together for the night. It was eleven thirty when Raymond and Sarah left the church to meet Christina.

Shirley and I waited for them to exit the church parking lot before we left for home. Considering the amount of stress the evening had provided—the discussions about personified evil and possible retaliation from Daniel—my wife and I felt great relief that the crisis had peaked and was on the downward side. As we drove home, Shirley filled me in on some of her conversation with Raymond and Sarah while I was talking to Officer Seaver near the church's entrance.

Our dominant thought was . . .*now what? We have rescued Raymond from the bad man. We have reunited him with his wife, but what will happen to them now?*

It seemed unavoidable that major difficulties would unfold in their relationship soon, even greater than before. One crisis had ended, but now another, perhaps more serious than Raymond's little adventure with Daniel, would form a stranglehold around each of their lives, as well as their marriage and family.

FAMILY RENDEZVOUS

As we were nearing home, Sarah and Raymond were connecting with their daughter. Christi entered the designated parking lot and parked her car next to her father's van. When she came to a stop, they all got out of their respective seats, met behind Christi's car, and hugged. It was the sweetest and most tender moment the Gils had experienced as a family in many years.

After this, they climbed into Christina's car to head for the hotel. Hers was the only vehicle they could all fit into. Raymond's van had a driver and passenger seat, but the rest of the van was filled with tools and construction materials. Raymond sat in the passenger seat and Christina was driving, while Sarah sat in the back.

Just before she started the car, Christina reached her hand over her seat to a spot between where her father was sitting and where her mother sat in the back and asked, "Well?"

Both her mom and Raymond were clueless.

Christina stiffened her arm, but still holding it in the same position questioned again, "Well?"

Her mom asked softly, "Well what, dear?"

Christina said scolding them, "Aren't we going to thank God for what He has done?"

Raymond and Sarah, both ashamed for different reasons, put their hands in their daughter's hand and Sarah said, "You're right, Christi. What's the matter with us?"

Then Sarah prayed, "Heavenly Father, thank You for bringing our daddy back home to us. Thank You for keeping us all safe. And I pray for your hedge of protection to be around all of us tonight. Bless Officer Jay for his kindness to us, and the excellent job he did to keep Raymond safe and encourage him to leave Daniel. You are a faithful God. Thank You for Your faithfulness to us. Amen."

After they prayed, Christina started the car, and drove to the hotel.

That was Day Six.

DAY SEVEN
FRIDAY

The day started early with Raymond's cell phone ringing in the hotel room. Raymond rolled over in his bed and looked to see who it might be. The caller ID displayed "PAY PHONE," hinting the caller was Daniel. Raymond was reluctant to answer it since both Sarah and Christina were in the room, not to mention his fear of talking to the shunned lover. He pushed the end call button on the phone's keypad and rolled back over in his bed, but he was wide-awake.

The phone rang a second time, a third, and then a fourth. Each time, Raymond aborted the call by quickly pressing the red button on his cell. Not wanting to arouse his family anymore, he grabbed the phone, slipped into the bathroom, closed the door, and waited for the next series of rings. But Daniel didn't call back, at least not right away.

The truth was, as much as Raymond was deathly afraid of Daniel and finally out of his grasp, he was still under his power. Blindly, Raymond still felt love for him. He also felt sorry for the man since he was in the throes of Raymond's rejection and police warnings to leave the Gils alone. But mostly, Raymond truly believed that as much as Daniel's control was very real, he himself was responsible for the relationship moving along as far as it did. He was taking ownership for the ordeal and feeling bad for Daniel's plight—without a lover, without a job, without a future…again. Daniel had lost and Raymond was feeling guilty about it.

The phone's ringing had awakened Sarah and Christina, and they began stirring. All three set themselves to the task of getting ready to leave the hotel. Christina had to go to work that morning at her department store. Raymond and Sarah needed to go to the police station to amend the restraining order. None of them took showers, figuring they would clean up at home. They picked up things and headed for the hotel parking lot.

As they prepared to open Christi's car doors, Raymond's phone rang again. They all knew who it was.

Raymond looked at Sarah and said, "He's going to keep calling until I pick it up. I might as well answer it and get it over with."

Sarah sneered, rolled her eyes, and said, "Fine! But this is the last time you are going to talk to that creep." As she and Christina were stepping into the car, she blurted out, "Make sure you tell him he is going to get a visit from the police today."

Raymond answered his phone while standing alone behind Christina's car.

Daniel began in a sympathetic tone: "Raymond, please don't hang up. Listen, I guess I didn't know how uncomfortable you were. I'm sorry for everything. I thought you really loved me. I guess I was wrong."

The mercy in Raymond's heart blurted out, "I do love you, Daniel," as his eyes glanced through the rear window to make sure Sarah and Christina were still in their seats.

But Daniel interrupted, "No, you don't have to say anything. I know it was too hard for you to leave your family. I should have known you could never have left Christina. And Sarah… well…I guess she won."

"Just don't worry about me," Daniel continued. "I'm going to transfer my parole and go back east and start a new life with my relatives. Remember I told you about my family back there? I already called them, and they said they would be more than happy to put me up and get me started. It won't be for a few months, though. It takes some time to transfer a parole. Is there any way I could still work for you for a while, because I don't have any money?"

As Raymond listened, he felt bad, but he was also greatly relieved.

"Listen, Daniel," responded Raymond. "I don't think that would work very well. But I'm sorry about how all of this turned out. I guess neither of us could foresee the problems."

"Raymond," said Daniel. "I need to go now. Maybe I'll drop you a note sometime. Good-bye, and for what it's worth...I love you, too."

Daniel didn't give Raymond a chance to comment. He just hung up.

Raymond thought Daniel's hurry to hang up seemed a bit peculiar. But on the other hand, Raymond was so relieved he was feeling almost giddy. He jumped into Christi's car with a big smile on his face.

He said, "Well, I am glad I answered that call. He is going back east to his parent's home. He's leaving in a few months, as soon as he can get his parole transferred. He'll be three thousand miles away and we'll never see him again."

Sarah didn't respond as positively to the good news as her husband did. Still focused on the task at hand she asked, "But we are still going to the police station to add names to the restraining order, right?"

"Most definitely," said Raymond. But inside he felt it wasn't necessary. After all, Daniel was on his way out of town—even out of the state.

Raymond phoned me from Christina's car to let me know of Daniel's new plans and to find out, if and when Shirley and I would be at the church. I was not particularly happy Raymond had answered a call from Daniel either, but even over the phone I could sense Raymond's lightheartedness with Daniel's decision to leave the area. So, I didn't pursue my discomfort with him.

Christina dropped her mom and dad off where they had parked the van the night before and left for home to shower and get ready for work. Though she was intent on not owning any fear of Daniel, she was also quite relieved the crisis had reached a peaceful end. She felt a little like a new day was dawning for her family.

Sarah, though a little more cautious, was feeling as if a huge burden had been lifted off her as well. In the back of her mind, she knew she and Raymond had a big battle to fight for their marriage, but that future and certain tussle wasn't taking the joy away from the smaller victory they had just won. She too was feeling that a significant hurdle was behind them.

I was feeling a bit relieved as well. I had awakened that morning joyful and ready to tackle the day. I arrived at the church early so that I could affect some finishing touches on my Sunday message. Shirley came soon after me in our other car because she had some work to do in preparation for the weekend as well. That is where I received Raymond's phone call from Christina's car, reporting the good news about Daniel's move back east. The call from Raymond had the "ring of relief" attached to it for me as well.

This was going to be a big day for us. Allen, a new staff member, was going to begin work at the church this very day, and both Shirley and I were excited about it. Allen wasn't coming in until later, but I wanted to get some work out of the way so I could spend some quality orientation time with him. I felt, especially with the Gil crisis behind us, the day was going to be a welcomed reprieve from the stress of the past week.

We were definitely through with Daniel.

When Christina dropped her mom and dad off at his van, they hopped in and drove straight to the police station. They wanted to make sure they made the necessary changes to the restraining order before it would be served to Daniel.

No Fear Again

Meanwhile, Christina arrived home, took a quick shower, put on some makeup and fresh clothes, and scooted out of the house. When she opened her car door Daniel startled her. He had stepped out from behind a large tree in their front lawn and surprised Christi, so she uttered a gasp.

"Where are your mom and dad?" Daniel asked Christi as lightheartedly as his sinister emotions would allow.

Having collected herself from the surprise, she answered bravely and sternly, "That's none of your business."

"That's bold talk for a little girl, isn't it?" Daniel asked sarcastically.

"Listen, Daniel," Christi shot back. "I don't know who you think you are, but you don't scare me. And just so you know, the police are looking for you." Then she said sharply, "I've got to go to work, so good-bye."

She whirled around and slid into the driver's seat of her car as she slammed the door. She started the engine and peeled backwards out of her driveway, leaving Daniel standing alone in the Gil front yard.

Christina's store opened at ten in the morning, but cashiers needed to arrive early enough to reconcile their drawers, organize their counters, and prepare their stations for transactions.

Meantime, Raymond and Sarah were making headway on adding several names and all the places they frequent to the restraining order. They were told the order would be served as early as that morning, as long as Daniel was at home to receive it. They took nearly an hour to work through the procedures required to amend the order.

While Christina was preparing her front counter, the other checker in the booth beside her tapped her on the shoulder and said, "Christi, who is that weirdo outside? He looks like some kind of lunatic or something."

In response, Christina turned around and looked out the front window. There in front of the building was Daniel.

The whole front of the store was glass and faced the parking lot in a large strip mall and was situated between two major chains. Daniel was pacing up and down the sidewalk in front of the full length of the store. He wasn't looking in at Christina. He was just walking, deliberately and briskly with his head down, like he was lost in some mental maze. He was going back and forth . . . back and forth.

Christina looked in disgust at Daniel and responded to her workmate, "Don't even waste your time. I think he *is* nuts. He's just some idiot my father knows. Just ignore him."

She didn't know how he got there so quickly from her house, but Christina turned her back and continued to ready her checkout stand for the day. A few minutes later, however, she did glance over her shoulder to see if Daniel was still acting like a caged lion in front of the store. But he was gone. She walked over to the window, looked to the right and the left, but saw no sign of Daniel.

A few minutes later the store opened.

When finished at the police station, Raymond and Sarah exited the front doors and headed for the van. They were feeling like they had a new lease on life.

As they got into Raymond's van, Sarah said, "Do you think it would be a good idea to go over to Christina's store, just to be sure she is all right?"

"I don't know," said Raymond. "I guess it wouldn't hurt."

Raymond was still ashamed in front of his wife. But he was humbled that she had made the kind of effort she had the week prior, to rescue him from what she perceived to be a dangerous situation. Without being too presumptuous, he hoped it represented a desire in her heart to stay with him. As they drove, they talked about things they needed to do… but not their relationship. That subject, they both knew, was a discussion for another time.

I was fast at work, feeling both peace and a sense of satisfaction that "Operation Save Raymond" had been a smashing success. I think it was Raymond's words and joyful demeanor over the phone earlier that had me breathing much easier and feeling especially unburdened. It also felt good to be back to normal with my wife tending the outer office and me at my desk preparing for the weekend.

By this time, Christina had forgotten about Daniel, since he had apparently left his post in front of the store.

But Daniel wasn't gone. He had left the store just long enough to cross the street, enter another store, and make a purchase. On the way back he grabbed a soda at a nearby fast food establishment and returned to Christina's workplace. There he stood behind a pillar outside the store…and waited.

A group of junior high students entered the clothing store while on a field trip from school and stood near the front a few yards away from Christina's checkout stand.

When Daniel saw that Christina was distracted and had her back to the front door, he slipped from his hideout behind the pillar, quickly entered the store through the glass doors and turned to the right toward Christina's booth. He leaped over the counter onto Christina's back and began stabbing her; violently, angrily, mercilessly, relentlessly; with the ten-inch kitchen knife he had just bought.

And as he stabbed, he screamed, "It's not my fault. It's not my fault. Call your dad and thank him for this. It's his fault Christi is dead."

Christina's checkout partner watched in horror as she frantically backed away. Of the junior high students standing nearby, some turned and ran to the back of the store and hid behind racks of clothes. Some ran straight out the rear fire escape door. Others just backed away as they watched . . . paralyzed with fear.

It seemed that Daniel's slaughter would never end. Over and over he raised his arm thrusting the blade into Christina's back and side, screaming like a madman and shouting profanities and accusations toward Raymond as he did. Sixteen times he thrust the weapon into Christina's helpless body penetrating vital organs in her torso five different times.

Christina had no chance. She tried to fight back, but Daniel was too strong and too emotionally charged for a small-framed teenager like Christina to be able to ward off an attack such as he was mounting. She was too weak to resist or run before she even realized what was happening to her. By the time Daniel withdrew the murderous blade from Christina's body for the sixteenth and final time, she lay motionless. Then, as if his fury were yet unsatisfied, while straddling her lacerated and bleeding back, Daniel reached in front of her head, grabbed her chin, stretched her neck to its limits, and slashed her throat from side to side. It wasn't even necessary. Christina was dead before the knife ever touched her neck.

Spectators watched horrified. No one dared intervene. Daniel was so frenzied and maniacal; interference would have meant certain death for the mediator as well. He massacred the beautiful life called Christina Gil as a wild beast would an animal of prey.

When Daniel's deed was finished, he stood up. He was dripping in Christina's blood from his head to his toes.

Satisfied his bloody task was complete, he gazed around at the terrified and petrified onlookers, held his hand straight out in front of him, and dropped the knife. It fell to the floor with a thud that would echo in the minds of those who heard it forever.

As if he hadn't made his point while stabbing, Daniel shouted again loudly for all in earshot to hear as he gazed around at his shocked audience, "It's not my fault that she's dead. Her father made her the person she was. Ask Raymond Gil who killed his daughter." Then Daniel calmly slipped outside the store, sat down on the curb, and waited for the police to arrive.

With the murderer gone from the inside of the store, a good Samaritan with medical training jumped on top of Christina's body and began trying to put pressure on her wounds to stop the bleeding. But Christina's wounds were too massive—too numerous—and her body was already void of life. The lady quickly discerned that no hope remained. She stood and backed away.

The front inside of the store around Christina's counter was draped in her blood. Her lifeless body lay face down in the middle of it with red footprints from Daniel and the good-Samaritan leading out from the pool surrounding the tragic scene. It was a gruesome sight.

Someone walking by saw the blood all over Daniel, and, unaware of what had just occurred, asked him, "What happened?"

"I killed her," Daniel spouted back. "Thank her father. It's not my fault. It was her dad who made her the person she was." Then as if primed by the lady's question and still sitting and covered with Christina's blood, Daniel began to spew curses and additional blame toward Raymond. He spoke to himself—but loud enough for people to hear—like a crazy man possessed by a demon.

Shortly after this, the police arrived in several cars all screeching to a halt in front of the building. They exited their cars cautiously with pistols drawn, all aimed at the blood-covered man sitting on the curb. But resistance was not in Daniel's plans. His vengeance complete, he raised his hands, looked at them and repeated calmly, "It's not my fault. Ask Raymond Gil whose fault it is." Then Daniel Rogers surrendered without a fight.

IRONIC THANK YOU

Raymond and Sarah had decided not to go to Christina's work, figuring it wasn't necessary. They would check on their daughter later. Instead, they headed for home. Raymond dropped Sarah off, because he had an errand to run. Sarah went into the house and checked her answer machine. The display said there was one call. She pushed the button, but all she could hear was noise, people's voices, faint screams, and things falling. It sounded as if someone was making a prank call. She just erased it and sat down to think. But she felt strangely uneasy, not about the odd message . . . just everything.

How could she have known the message was from Christina? Somehow, as Daniel's hatred and knife were piercing her body, and while she was battling for her life, she fell to the floor and reached for her phone on the lower shelf of her checkout stand. Apparently, she pushed the quick dial button in an effort to communicate with the only people she knew to call in an emergency. By the time the answer device at home had taken the call, Christina's body was too weak to respond—almost lifeless—almost gone. Though uneasy, Sarah had no idea the call was from Christina and no idea of her daughter's plight.

When Raymond dropped Sarah off, he went to the grocery store to buy a bouquet of flowers and then came over to the church. He wanted to give the flowers to my wife and thank both of us for saving his life.

I could see Raymond through the door as he entered the outer office and handed the flowers to Shirley. There was an exchange of appreciation and hugs. Immediately after his *thank you* was spoken; the church phone rang. I answered it. It was Sarah.

She asked in a panicked voice, "Is Raymond there?"

"Yes," I answered. "What's wrong, Sarah?"

"I don't know. I don't know." She said nervously. "But I just got a call from Christina's work, and they said something's happened to Christina. She's been hurt or something. Could you tell Raymond to come home right away?"

"We'll be right there," I told her, and hung up the phone.

"Raymond," I blurted out as I rose from my desk and headed toward the front office where Shirley and Raymond were. "That was Sarah, and she just received a call from Christina's store. Something's happened to Christina."

As Raymond and I bolted out the church door for my car, I said to Shirley, "Call some people to pray."

In that instant, I knew Daniel had taken his vengeance out on Christina. And I knew she was dead.

The terror in Raymond's heart wouldn't allow him the same discernment. As we ran to my car and drove to his house, Raymond kept asking frantic, yet hopeful, questions like, "What do you think happened? Do you think Daniel hurt her? Did they say she was all right?" But I didn't have any answers for him.

When we entered the Gil's front door, Sarah, hurriedly and with great concern, said, "I just got a call from the police. They said Christina has been injured and for us to stay here until we hear from them. I asked if she was all right, but they wouldn't tell me."

We waited for about three minutes. That's all! Then I said, "This is ridiculous. We need to go—now!"

I ushered them out the door, into my car, and we sped to the store. All the way, Raymond and Sarah were on the edge of their seats. "Do you think she's OK? They would have told us if she wasn't, right?" I tried to offer encouragement to their hopeful pleas, but I knew. Don't ask me how . . . I just knew.

When we pulled into the parking lot it was filled with police cars, all with lights flashing. A crowd of sizeable proportions had gathered in front of the department store and men and women dressed in blue were everywhere.

I parked the car and we ran toward the store. We were stopped by a group of officers and detectives and what I presumed were other police personnel dressed in civilian clothes.

"We are Christina Gil's mother and father," Raymond said. "Can we please go in?"

A few of the officers glanced at me, so I added, "I'm their pastor."

"No," said one of the detectives. "No one is being allowed entrance."

I was standing directly beside Raymond with my arm around his shoulder and Sarah was on the other side of Raymond.

Raymond asked, frenzied and with as much hope as he could muster under the circumstances, "Is Christina all right? Is my daughter alive?"

One detective stepped forward and said as sympathetically as he could, "I'm very sorry to tell you Mr. Gil . . . Mrs. Gil . . . your daughter is deceased."

"Ohhhhhh," Raymond wailed from the innermost recesses of his soul. He spun around, and falling onto my shoulder, began to sob and lament loudly. "What have I done? What have I done? I've killed my daughter."

With my eyes also dripping with tears, I looked over at Sarah. She had her hand on Raymond's back, but she was staring straight ahead. As I looked at her, she also turned her head to look at me. But she wasn't crying. She appeared emotionless, numb, paralyzed, stunned. Sarah's shock was back.

After Raymond's wailing subsided, he clumsily wiped his eyes and turned to ask the officer again, "Please sir, can my wife and I see our daughter?"

The detective said, "Mr. Gil, I understand why you would ask, but I can't permit anyone to go in there. First, it is not a sight you should see. But mostly, it is now a crime scene and only detectives are allowed to go in."

Seething with anger, I asked the detective, "Where is the man that did this? Where is Daniel Rogers? Did he get away?"

The detective said calmly, "We have Daniel Rogers in custody. After he finished with . . . the victim . . . he sat down on the curb and waited for us to get here. He gave himself up without resistance."

Then the detective turned to Raymond and Sarah and said, "I know there is no good news in any of this, but at least the one who did this is safely in custody."

Neither Raymond nor Sarah showed any emotion at the officer's announcement, as if it didn't matter. And it didn't, at least not to Raymond and Sarah. They didn't have the presence of mind to think of revenge or capture, or even their own safety.

It did matter to me, though. I asked the detective, "Where is Daniel? Is he in one of the police cars around here?"

Maybe I wanted to find him and taunt him or communicate to him how much I hated him right then. Perhaps I wanted to call him the monster I thought him to be. Or maybe, for the Gil's sake, I just wanted to be sure he was gone, and therefore, nowhere near them. The feelings I had for Daniel Rogers at that moment weren't at all holy.

But be sure, Daniel Rogers was anything but holy. It seems when the police took him into custody; he was full of dastardly information that gushed forth as a broken sewer main would spew sewage.

Daniel's sickening and unremorseful confessions to them went something like this:

"I never intended to leave the area. If Raymond had half a brain, he would have realized I wasn't going to do that. No, I was just trying to mislead them, kind of lull them to sleep. When that cop told me Thursday night there was going to be a restraining order out on me, I knew I had to work fast. But I will say; I never intended to just kill Christi. That was a last-minute brainstorm. Last night, I was going to kill the whole family. I wished I had a gun. It would have made it easy. But I didn't, so I went there figuring I would find whatever

weapon I could to do the job. I had a little knife with me. It wasn't really big enough to do much damage, but I would have made it work if I had seen them. But no one came home. So, I went there this morning. I was going to make sure I killed at least Raymond and Sarah, even if Christi wasn't there."

Daniel went on without remorse:

When I got there, Christi came out of the house and got testy with me, and I figured, why not kill her? I really hate her. Then, after she left for work, I thought, Yeah, that's the perfect plan. Raymond loves Christi more than Sarah. She is his pride and joy. If I kill her, Raymond will not only be without her from here on out, he will blame himself for her death until he dies, and so will everyone else...including Sarah. I've been telling Raymond if he left me, he would be sorry forever. I don't know why he didn't get it. I told him I would make him pay dearly if he ever left me. As I thought about it, I decided it was ingenious. I didn't care whether I spent the rest of my life in prison. I had spent the last several years there, anyway. I kind of knew my way around the place. It was worth it to me. So, I changed my mind right there in front of the Gil's house. I would butcher Christina. I would cut her up into little pieces. That way Raymond would have to live with that picture for the rest of his life."

His last statement, however, was the most chilling of all. Snickering, he said,

"I only have one-regret, and that is: I didn't get to see the look on Raymond's face when he first learned his beloved daughter was dead."

Minus fifty or so expletives, that is approximately what Daniel Rogers said to the officers that day. Then, when he arrived at the police station, he repeated it all again in a second equally coldhearted statement to detectives. And as he confessed, before they allowed him to wash it off, they made him sit with Christina's blood on his body while they took samples for forensic testing. Truly, Christina's blood was upon his hands.

STATEMENTS

A few minutes after my question about Daniel's whereabouts, a detective approached us about coming to the police station to make statements.

We piled into cars and drove the five or six blocks from the department store parking lot to the police station. In the car, I called Shirley and told her the awful news—news, to her chagrin, she also had already suspected. I told her we were going to the police station, and Sarah especially would need her comfort.

Shirley left the church immediately and drove to the police department. Upon arriving, we were asked to wait in the front foyer until rooms and personnel could be made available to meet with us. As we waited, Shirley also came into the waiting area. We were then ushered in to separate rooms with different detectives. The officers proceeded to take statements from each of us individually concerning the details of the past week leading up to Christina's murder.

My interview took more than an hour, as did each of the others. When finished, I was told mine was only a preliminary statement, and I would be called by an officer the next day to set up an appointment for a more exhaustive interview. I guess, in my initial interrogation, they wanted to assess whether my testimony would have anything to offer to the case. Apparently, it did.

It took nearly four hours to work through the red tape involved with the police department. When we were finished, I drove Raymond and Sarah home.

Raymond was on suicide watch. People at the police station had taken Shirley and I aside and warned us to monitor his emotions and state of mind closely.

From the time he learned of Christina's death, Raymond kept saying the same words over and over again. "What have I done? I've killed my daughter. I've killed my Christina. How can I live?" He inserted this lament between every few sentences when he spoke to Sarah, police officers, acquaintances or me. Like a broken record he would repeat the same mournful confession; and it went on that way for days.

It was interesting to me that from the time of Christina's murder, Raymond owned an incredible amount of responsibility for his daughter's death. A part of me knew exactly why. I certainly could see the connection with what he did and what had happened to Christina, as could everyone else; but I wasn't blaming Raymond. I was blaming Daniel. I wondered, however, if Raymond's extreme ownership in the matter had anything to do with his tendency to protect Daniel by hiding his threats from the police. Was Raymond feeling an extra dose of responsibility, because his blind love for Daniel foolishly compelled him to protect his parolee lover, leaving the madman on the streets?

Then there were Daniel's threatening words to Raymond. They were harrowing words, repeated to us the night before by Raymond in my office. "If you don't stay with me," Daniel said, "you will be sorry for the rest of your life." I had an idea Daniel said even worse than that to Raymond, but Raymond was sheltering Daniel for some reason. Yet, even those words were frightening. And now they seemed to be ringing true with Raymond. It could be Daniel's control had seeped into Raymond's consciousness and had convinced him of his guilt in his daughter's death.

By this time, a few people had informed Raymond of Daniel's words during and after his murder of Christina. "It's Raymond's fault she's dead." Perhaps Raymond believed

Daniel, and that is why Raymond was admitting so much liability in the matter.

Whatever was behind Raymond's desire to place the blame for Christina's death onto his own shoulders, though it seemed a little extreme to me, it was also good for Raymond, because it helped people to feel less angry with him. Frankly, it was the only thing allowing any mercy at all to flow from others to him. Still, others hearing about what had happened were very satisfied to aim responsibility in Raymond's direction. For Raymond to have shifted the blame elsewhere would have brought enormous judgment down upon him from every direction.

All these thoughts about blame in Christina's death unveil a bizarre and twisted kind of blame-shifting that was going on and was leaving minds reeling and confused about who was actually at fault. Oddly, many people, Raymond included, were not pointing fault in the proper direction.

Daniel Rogers was the murderer. Yet, it seemed everyone, including Raymond himself, was pointing the finger at Christina's father as the culprit.

How was I going to convince Raymond he wasn't worthy of sole blame—especially since so many were joining in on the accusations? Yes, he shouldn't have gotten into a relationship with a sordid character. And he shouldn't have left his wife. And Raymond's choice to experiment with the gay lifestyle was untimely and played into the mix; and there were other foolish and costly decisions he made as well. But no, he didn't decide he wanted his daughter dead, and he didn't wield the knife. But convincing Raymond of this was another story.

Soon after arriving at the Gil home, Shirley joined us and we spent a fair amount of time with Raymond and Sarah trying to comfort them, an impossible task given the circumstances, after which we went over to the church. By then, it was late afternoon. To say I was frazzled would have been a gross understatement.

I looked at my sermon and determined quickly it wouldn't be appropriate for Sunday now. In fact, I wasn't sure anything would.

My mind wandered to the front of the store where Christi's life came to an end, and I wondered . . . *Was she still there? No . . . I* thought . . . *It is five hours later. They must have taken her away by now.*

And I began to cry. Soon I was crying harder...and then harder with my head on my desk. For several minutes, I wept loudly, emotionally unaware of my surroundings. I wasn't sure whether it was from stress or sorrow or both. But it seemed I released everything that had been bottled up inside me since the Saturday before.

When I came to myself, I recalled the words I spoke over and over to Sarah and Christina . . . *We don't know what Daniel is capable of* . . . And I thought...*well, we know now, don't we?*

I also thought of Christina's words, "Daniel doesn't scare me. I'm not afraid of him."

And I thought . . . *Oh, Christina. You should have been afraid. You should have been very afraid.*

Just about then, Raymond came bursting through my office door and said, "Chris, I have to tell the people what I have done."

"Pardon me," I said. "What do you mean?"

While leaning over my desk, Raymond repeated, "I have to tell the people in our church what I've done. I have to confess everything I did and ask for their forgiveness. They may not want to forgive me, and I wouldn't blame them for that. But I have to tell them. And I have to tell them this Sunday I can't wait. What do you think?"

Raymond surprised me, and I stuttered a bit, "Well . . . I . . . I . . . don't know. It may be very appropriate considering what has happened. But . . . let me run it by our elders."

Raymond had certainly caught me off guard, but the truth was I wasn't sure anything else would fly anyway. Probably by then, the whole church had heard about what happened, maybe the whole city. Nothing else was coming to me for Sunday, and the people of our church needed and deserved an explanation. Everything we had slated was no longer suitable.

"Raymond," I said. "I'll tell you what; go home to be with your wife. I think your heart to share the truth is commendable. I'll get back with you as soon as I talk to our leadership."

So, Raymond left for home.

After I had a chance to think about it, Raymond's idea seemed to be the most appropriate direction for our church service, which would take place only two days from then. I just wasn't sure how the people in our church would respond. In fact, I was quite uneasy as I thought about what might happen. Would people walk out on Raymond as he spoke; or challenge him publicly? I certainly didn't want that to happen.

In response to my messages, each of my elders called me at the church and with one voice agreed, in light of what had happened, Raymond was supposed to share his confession with the church.

It wasn't that they felt what Raymond did required the punishment of having to confess his transgression. It was that the church was worthy of an explanation.

Our church was where Raymond had professed a relationship with Christ, and where he, his wife, and daughter had worshiped God for years. The Gils had committed their loyalty to this group of people, and the church had committed theirs to the Gils. Raymond's compulsion to confess, our elders felt, was God's direction for Raymond's sanity and healing, and what was proper considering the church's place in his life and the lives of his family.

Furthermore, it was a New Testament directive, and therefore, reflected the sovereign wisdom of God (1 Tim. 5:20). We were all convinced Raymond's strong desire to come clean with our church the following Sunday was God's plan.

By this time, it was into the evening of the day Christina was murdered. Instead of calling Raymond with the elder's response, I decided to go to their home to tell them face-to-face.

They had begun to call relatives to inform them of the tragedy, a horrible exercise because of all the grief it kept before them, and the explanations they were forced to give. I pulled them away from their painful task to talk with them.

As we sat down in their living room, Raymond began to voice his lament again. "Chris, what have I done? I've killed my precious little girl. How can I go on living?" Then he broke into tears.

I looked over at Sarah. She was stone-faced. Not from anger, though. The shock of the last week had hit its peak. Her daughter was dead. No emotions would come.

Trying to console him, she said, "Raymond. It's OK. No, you didn't. You have much to live for."

Then she looked at me and said, "He's been saying this over and over all day."

I took a few minutes to offer what comforting words came to my mind, but I had a sense Raymond's laments would not be ending any time soon.

At a certain point, I began to realize that Raymond's deep groans were quite necessary. Even if they represented other repressed issues we knew nothing about, at the very least, they were serving as a kind of penance Raymond was imposing upon himself—a type of punishment that helped him endure the pain.

It could be his desire to tell the whole church was a similar act of contrition (only on a much larger scale) that Raymond hoped would move him closer to a place of absolution and would eliminate some of the pain he felt. Whatever Raymond's reason for wanting to tell the church about what he did and own the blame for his daughter's death, it was apparent it was in God's plan, because all our church leadership, with one voice, felt it was right.

When Raymond finished his moment of remorse, I informed him that our elders had agreed it would be good for him to make a confession to the church on Sunday morning. I talked with him and Sarah about how we would structure it in the service. Then I prayed with them and left. It was after nine when I walked out their door.

All the way home, Shirley in her car and I in mine, I had it out with God.

"Why?" I shouted at Him. "What are You doing in all of this? How can You bring good out of a tragedy such as this?"

I wept. I screamed. I voiced my utter disapproval of His methods. I registered my concern that He really may not know what He is doing. I aired my grievances. I was so emotional as I drove, with tears gushing from my eyes, it's a wonder I arrived home in one piece.

I drove into my garage, shut the door, told my wife I had no conversation ability left, and went to bed.

That was Day Seven, and what a day it was! No day in the ministry, past or future, could ever compare with this one—or so I thought.

DAY EIGHT
SATURDAY

I had challenged God Himself the night before, but by Saturday morning, as I lay awake in my bed, I found myself questioning His Word.

I had been a pastor for nearly thirty years. I prepared for and preached a Bible sermon almost every Sunday for all that time; and for many years, every Sunday night and Wednesday night as well. I had read through the Old and New Testaments multiple times and had worn out several Bibles. My only regret was that I didn't know God's Word better. I had always trusted its wisdom and guidance for every situation in my life, my family's lives, and the lives of those God had called me to lead in the ministry. Everything I learned and every truth I discovered from the Bible had never shaken my trust in God's Word but had only strengthened it—until I witnessed the events of Day Seven.

This Saturday morning, I was having a difficult time understanding several scriptures. Interestingly, they were verses I had used over the years to help me trust. Now they were shaking my trust as I pondered the events of the past week.

I knew well the text in Romans 8:28: *"And we know that all things work together for good to those who love God, to those who are called according to <u>His</u> purpose"* (emphasis added). I had taught it with what I thought was theological prowess on many occasions. But this morning I was having a hard time seeing how God could apply its message to Christina's death and the Gil family. The crisis was too tragic, too shocking, too confusing, and too painful. How could any good come from this?

I John 4:4 tells *us "He who is in you is greater than he who is in the world."* When I thought of Daniel jumping over that counter at Christi's store and snatching the life away from our little girl, I found myself wondering about who was greater—the One who was in me or the one who was in the world? Did God have any control over Daniel's fury, or did He choose to not intervene? Either way, He seemed unlike the God the Bible describes.

The Book of Job tells us that when Satan sought to take Job's life, God forbade it (Job 2:6). This day I was questioning, "Why didn't God forbid it for Christina?" The church elders were praying. Sarah was praying. Shirley and I were praying. Some others who knew were praying. And we were all praying for safety for each one in the family. Why had Satan's query come across God's desk concerning Christina's life requesting he take it, and God's answer came forth… Yes? Why?

Psalm 91 contains comforting information about God's promises to protect His children. The scripture says that God will bear us up should we dash our feet against a stone. He will deliver us from the snare and the fowler, and no evil shall befall us. It promises protection under His wings from the arrow that flies by day, the pestilence that walks in darkness, and the destruction that lays waste at noonday. But it seemed this segment of God's Word didn't work for Christina. Nor did it work for Raymond and Sarah who were perhaps as much destroyed by Christina's death as she was.

I also wondered about the power of prayer. *"And whatever things you ask in prayer, believing, you will receive"* (Matthew 21:22). But this verse didn't seem to apply to Christina and her family either. Sarah's prayers, our prayers, our elder's prayers, and the prayers of many others, all seemed to fall dead.

Now I knew, as the head of his family, over the years Raymond had not conducted himself as admirably as he should have. I knew he had set a poor example of moral integrity, obedience to God, and submission to his spiritual leaders. He had also modeled a critical attitude before his entire family and had not been diligent to pray God's protection over them.

Had God decided He had enough of Raymond's shenanigans, and it was time for him to pay a price? Had God finally dropped the gauntlet on Raymond? I wasn't convinced from what I knew of Scripture, that this was an accurate description of the character of our God. I knew of much more righteous people who had very difficult things happen to them; and I knew of much less righteous people who had no real or comparable crises happen to them.

I had spoken on the consequences of sin many times. Was this merely a consequence of Raymond's pursuit of a questionable lifestyle, Christina's pride and a lack of godly fear? Had they just suffered consequences for their actions? Yet, wasn't Sarah's trust of God her whole life and throughout the last week enough to get God's attention to appropriate His protection?

Nothing made sense to me scripturally or cognitively considering what I knew about God. Theologically, I was forced to resort to blind faith. While nothing made sense as I examined all that had occurred, it seemed that to make sense of any of it my trust of God and His sovereignty had to remain in the equation. So, though confused, I trusted Him, believing in the end I would begin to discern God's hand in all of it.

My plan was to wake up early, go to the church, and prepare a whole new message for Sunday designed around an introduction for Raymond's confession. I forgot about the more detailed statement the police wanted to take from me that day. However, remembrance came back to me like an electric shock to my brain when my phone rang at seven twenty and startled me out of my horizontal theological ponderings.

It was a lady from the police department. She wanted to meet with me at my house to record my testimony. I was so groggy I agreed without protest. When I hung up, I lay there in my bed for about five seconds before I realized my blunder.

I threw my covers off in a panic.

"What's wrong?" my wife shouted, thinking the phone call represented another emergency equal to the one the day before.

I said, "I forgot about the police wanting to talk to me again today. But I have to go to the church and write a whole new sermon for tomorrow. A lady from the police department is meeting me here at the house at eleven. They don't want to tape it at the church, because they want to avoid possible interruptions. I've got to get going."

I took a quick shower, got dressed, hopped into my car, squealed out of the driveway and headed for church.

I seem to work well under pressure. I guess the urgency helps me focus. I worked for two solid hours and made good headway. After I felt confident that I was prepared for the next day's unusual service, I went over to the Gil's to check on them.

Upon arriving Raymond asked me if I would call four specific families who were friends and who didn't attend our church, one being the chiropractor who had helped on Tuesday and Wednesday. He wanted me to ask them to be at the church service in the morning to hear what he was going to say. Raymond's feeling was he would need to tell the story and confess his mistakes to them anyway. He wanted me to call them, because he feared they would press him for details. He would rather tell everyone all at once. I agreed to make the calls.

I said my good-byes to Raymond and Sarah, told them I would be in touch with them later, and headed home. I arrived just in time to meet the police detective who would be recording my statement.

I went through the account with her again, but this time more analytically.

This was my third time experiencing the story.

The *first* was the experience itself. It was a weeklong encounter with the event. It was filled with anticipation, fear, despair, pain, second guessing, a myriad of decisions, and moves, and strategies we attempted to use to rescue Raymond from danger and preserve the lives of those in the Gil family. We did all these things not knowing what the outcome might be. Sadly, Christina's murder became that tragic result. At every turn, this first experience was marked by surprise and uncertainty.

The *second* time I experienced it was when I told the story at the police station. In this experience, I had pieced together a general recap in a highly charged moment immediately following the unbelievable climax to the weeklong event. But I was flustered. As the police interviewed me, I was worried about Raymond and Sarah and their interviews. I was thinking about Christina and the terror she must have undergone. I was battling angry feelings toward Daniel, and I was feeling a great deal of my own personal pain as well. In short, during my second telling of the story there had not been time to process all that had taken place.

This *third* time telling the story was different. It was eye opening. I had the opportunity to take my time and go through the facts slowly and deliberately. I was able to analyze the events as they occurred, our interpretations of those events, the decisions we made and why, and make observations from an overview of what happened. Before, we were deep in the forest, unable to see it for the trees. By this time, however, I had stepped back and was able to see the whole story at once.

And for the first time, it hit me. It hit me like a slug in the gut.

I had failed. I had tried with every ounce of my being. I had interpreted the situation correctly as very perilous indeed. All we did, we did with the Gils's safety in mind. Everything!

And yet, I couldn't save Christina. I had taken charge, because I knew it was my place to do so, but I had failed. I had lost Christi. I recalled . . . *Why did we think we only needed to keep the Gils away from Daniel on Thursday night? Why didn't we have the presence of mind to realize Daniel's vengeance may not cool off with a night's sleep? How utterly foolish!*

As much as it was enlightening to tell the story a third time, it was also painful in its own way. The lady detective thanked me for my testimony and then left about twelve thirty that afternoon. But as the detective walked out the door, I found myself fighting back my emotions again. I closed the door, sat down on my couch, and began to weep again, almost as emotionally as I had the day before in my office. Over and over again, I confessed my failure as I wept. "I'm so sorry, Christina. I tried as hard as I could, but I failed. Forgive me. Please forgive me."

After my time of mourning I collected myself and hurried back to the church to work. Three chores needed attention: the calls to Raymond's friends, finishing touches on my sermon, and a complete alteration of the morning service. So, I set myself to the tasks.

MORE LAMENTS

At three o'clock that afternoon, Raymond walked into my office and sat on my couch. He said, "I called your house and Shirley said you were here."

I looked at Raymond sympathetically. I could tell he needed to talk. I couldn't imagine the pain he must have been feeling. All my problems, however difficult I saw them to be, seemed microscopic right then—including my need to complete my work for Sunday.

I rose from my seat behind my desk and sat in one of my counseling chairs in front of the couch across from where Raymond was sitting.

Looking back, I know now what he said to me that Saturday afternoon represented a kind of composite of all his pain, wrapped up into one lengthy and therapeutic monologue. He would speak these things repeatedly in fragmented episodes, in long and short emotional bursts, over the next few years, and, prophetically speaking, tapering off gradually for the rest of his life.

He began sorrowfully, thoughtfully, forcefully, painfully, tearfully, redundantly . . .

"I don't . . . I can't tell you to this day why I did what I did; why I didn't say, 'Sarah, this is what's been going on. Dan is asking me to leave with him. What do you want me to do?' Why didn't I say that? I . . . I . . I . . . I can't tell you."

"What I didn't want was the people, my customers, our friends, and the people in church to know what was going on. But the minute I did what I did, they would know. I cannot understand why I didn't realize that. I cannot understand why I didn't get up on Sunday morning, the next day after I left Sarah, and drive to church."

"I don't know why I told Christi what I told her—that I was going to live with Daniel, that I was gay, and that I would sell our house so her mother would be taken care of. She left crying."

"But he wouldn't let me talk to her by myself. Then, after she left, he said, 'She'll get over it. She's over it already.' I just cried."

"I was scared to death I would ruin my reputation. But it didn't sink into my head that as soon as I walked out on Sarah, everybody would know. I don't know why I couldn't get that. Why didn't I just drive away? Why didn't I just come back to my house and say, 'The heck with him?' I . . . I . . . I don't understand it. I think back and I say why? Why didn't I drive over to the church? Why didn't I drive over to the police station? Was he holding me by force? Did he have a gun to my head?"

"I was miserable. From the moment we left the house last Saturday night until Thursday night, I wasn't out of his sight for more than five minutes at a time. I couldn't even close the door to go to the bathroom."

"But I sit, and I think . . . and I think . . . and I think . . . and I think; why didn't I just leave? I can't answer that question and that's what bugs me so much. I mean, when I suggested to Sarah to ask you to meet me at the chiropractor's office, what was I expecting? What did I think would happen? I don't know. I really don't. Were you going to create a miracle that would get me out of the mess I was in? I don't know."

"During that period of time when we did intimate things, he literally forced me to do them with him. I was done. In fact, after a couple of weeks of doing those things after I first met him—maybe three weeks later—I was done. The newness, the excitement, was gone. I knew at that point it was wrong for me to keep going. But by then he had me."

"He started saying, 'If you don't do what I tell you, I'll tell your wife.' If I fought him on it, he'd get mad. And I would pray, *Lord, what should I do? Please put an end to this. I beg of You to take me out of this.*"

"When that policeman showed up Thursday night, I don't know how to express the feeling I had. I walked out there to the side with him. He didn't even start to talk to me, and I started bawling."

"Then he said, 'What's going on here Raymond?'"

"I said, 'I've gotten myself into something that I don't know how to get out of.'"

"I think back, and I keep repeating to myself, 'I can't understand why I didn't just walk away.' The van was locked all the time. But I could have grabbed the keys, run to the van, unlocked my side, jumped in, and driven off. I don't know why I didn't do that. I still don't know why I didn't do it. I mean, I could have done that Sunday morning and driven to the church. I could have done that Saturday night when I took him home. I could have jumped in my side of the van and driven to the house and said, 'Sarah, I've got to tell you something. I've got to tell you what's happening.' But I didn't."

By this time, Raymond was swimming in his own tears. I didn't know how to interrupt him. There wasn't one word I could think of that would be comforting, so I sat there just watching him, trying to hold back my own tears and attempting to feel his pain, but sensing I never could. Finally, I moved from my chair onto the couch beside him and put my arm around his shoulder. He leaned into me and just cried.

As Raymond sat with his head on my shoulder, I thought of what he had just said in his lengthy lament... *Truly there are great perils that occur when we are unable to share the truth in our lives with others; when the secrets of our thoughts and actions are so shameful to us, we feel we have to hide them from others at all costs. The entire Gil incident could have been averted if Raymond had just been in a place where he could have shared the truth of his behavior or errant feelings with others.*

I also thought about Raymond's words while he leaned against me as a child would a parent... *The excitement was gone... Of course the excitement is gone. The excitement of sin is always gone in a very short time.*

I also thought of Raymond's words during his lament... *When the sensual feelings were no longer there, that is when he knew it was wrong.* And I thought... *How many times have I instructed my church over the years; just because something feels good or right, doesn't make it good or right. Nor does it make it safe?' The righteousness of a thing is not determined by how it feels. That is one reason God gave the Ten Commandments (Galatians 3:19), so His children would have instruction and not have to rely on their deceptive feelings to show them what is right and wrong (Proverbs 14:12).*

I felt great despair for everything as I sat there holding this broken man. I felt that way largely because of all the reasoning

Raymond had used to make the decisions he made. They ultimately had plunged him into this tragedy of a lifetime, and they had all of us reeling.

All the very simple wisdom necessary for him to make the right decisions had been taught to Raymond, at the very least by me, if not other pastors prior to my induction into his life. Had my teachings been unclear? Had Raymond's attitude toward me caused him to refuse to hear? Did Raymond have a hard heart toward God and His Word, leaving him unable to hear or understand? Had my attitude toward Raymond persuaded him to resist the influence and meaning of my words?

Several minutes later he seemed to be cried out.

He sat up, sniffled a few times, and asked, "You know what happened to me this morning?"

"What?"

"Someone from the police department called me at the house and said, 'Mr. Gil, I'm trying to deliver this restraining order to Daniel Rogers, but he's never home. I can't serve it if I can't find him.'"

"Oh, you're kidding Raymond. What did you say?"

"I wasn't very nice," said Raymond. "I told him, 'What's the matter with you stupid people? It's too late. He's in jail, and my daughter is dead.' Then I hung up."

WOULD THE PAIN PLEASE STOP? I thought so loudly within myself I felt Raymond must have heard. *Can this family take any more suffering?*

I changed the subject so I wouldn't be tempted to voice unkind words about the police department. Then I prayed with him and he left for home.

I still had plenty to do, but I paused to think about what I had just witnessed with Raymond. What kind of evil must have been at work in Daniel to create that kind of terror, and now guilt, in Raymond?

I began to think . . . *how could one man, Daniel, allow such wickedness to enter his soul, let alone feel justified that it was there?* All kinds of thoughts were running through my head. I thought of all the statements made by characters involved in this horrendous drama that took place the previous week:

"He's threatening me and my family."

"I'll bash your head in."

"He wouldn't let me out of his sight."

"I don't know why I couldn't just leave."

"It's not my fault."

"We don't know what he is capable of."

"I'm not afraid of you."

"I'm moving back east."

I couldn't believe how duped we all had been. Daniel Rogers used lies, threats, manipulations, control, intimidation, terror, and finally murder, to overpower, not just Raymond, but all of us. Now he was in jail, but he was still wielding his evil power. Had we been dealing with the devil incarnate?

After my thoughts on these things subsided, I finished my work and left for home.

That was Day Eight

DAY NINE
SUNDAY

As is usual on Sundays, I woke up early to study for my sermon presentation. It would be different this day as my message, instead of being the main feature, was going to be an introduction to Raymond's confession to the church.

I was uneasy about what might happen that morning. I had presided over a few services where people had confessed certain failures to the church. Those services had gone remarkably well. The people who attended embraced the one confessing with love, acceptance and forgiveness. Their response had been a beautiful reflection of God's own compassion and mercy toward each of us. I think the success of those services was why I was quick to feel positive about Raymond making his confession to our church.

However, the nature and magnitude of Raymond's ordeal would take public confession to a whole new level.

The other incidents had not involved murder, as Raymond's had, or anything close; and a brutal and violent murder at that. Furthermore, it was someone in our church who was murdered—someone very dear to us.

In addition, as well as was her daughter, Sarah was a victim. She was the jilted wife and the grieving mother. Raymond was the bad guy. Daniel was out of the picture. The fact he wielded the knife could very well be a non-issue in the wake of Raymond's responsibility in the matter. It wasn't going to be just a confession of sin. Raymond was going to be explaining how his indiscretion had snatched one of our kids from us and had completely devastated a lady in our fellowship.

I was concerned because I had no idea what to expect from our church, and my concentration level while studying that morning was rather low.

Shirley and I arrived early so we could get some of the details of the service out of the way to free us to concentrate on the needs and questions of people. We also wanted to have plenty of time to instruct the ushers and other volunteer personnel on how to respond to different individuals as they arrived.

As the time for the beginning of our service drew near, it became apparent we would have a full house. A few visitors came that morning; but it seemed every person who called our church home, regular and periodic attendee alike, was in attendance this Sunday morning. But it wasn't curiosity that brought them. This was a family event. People just knew they should be there. In addition, the four families Raymond asked me to call, as well as a few others who knew the Gils were present at the service.

Also apparent as the service was about to begin, was the overall demeanor of those present. People were both solemn and concerned. None knew what they were going to encounter that morning, except perhaps the four families I contacted for Raymond. By then word had gotten around to many of some awful tragedy that had fallen upon the Gils. So, people were arriving in solemn anticipation of an explanation of what happened to them...and to Christina.

To complicate matters, the local newspapers and television stations, as well as nearby major network had gotten wind that the Gils went to our church, and that something may be said in our service about Christina's death. They had asked permission the day before to videotape our service, which we declined at Raymond's request. But we all knew this was not a time for public intrusion.

However, reporters and cameras were beginning to gather on our property as the service time approached. Anticipating this, I had instructed our ushers and elders to not permit them entry to our building to allow our church family privacy to process all that they would hear that morning. Due to the nature of what had happened, we also wanted to give Raymond and Sarah that degree of anonymity.

Raymond and Sarah did not sit in the main body of the auditorium. They arrived a little late, parked in the back of the church, and entered through the back door. The plan was: they would slip into my office and stay there until the service was well under way. Then they would enter the auditorium during the service so they wouldn't have to talk with people.

SERMONS

When it was time for me to speak, I stood at a podium in the center of our platform and told the people to turn to Romans 8:35–39, and I began to read.

> *"Who shall separate us from the love of Christ? Shall tribulation, or distress, or persecution, or famine, or nakedness, or peril, or sword? As it is written: "For Your sake we are killed all day long; we are accounted as sheep for the slaughter." Yet in all these things we are more than conquerors through Him who loved us. For I am persuaded that neither death nor life, nor angels nor principalities nor powers, nor things present nor things to come, nor height nor depth, nor any other created thing, shall be able to separate us from the love of God which is in Christ Jesus our Lord."*

When I finished reading, I looked out over the packed auditorium. You could hear a pin drop, and not a single movement could be detected.

I began.

"There is no greater news in the universe than the love of God. The fact that God loves us is world-class headline information. It brings comfort, peace, and solace in times of crisis, and when times are good, it will crown our heads with joy."

It was clear to me that this was not going to be a difficult message to give where people's attention was concerned. Every gaze was riveted on me.

I continued.

"Sometimes Christians will become judgmental of others—pointing fingers and making accusations about their unholy living. It's not anything new. The religious leaders of Jesus' day did the same thing to the Son of God himself. They brought people to Jesus, demanding that He stone them for their sin in keeping with their religious rules. They also criticized Jesus for socializing with sinners while they turned up their noses at people of unrighteous character."

About this time, I looked toward the window in the back door to our worship center and saw a face I didn't recognize... and then a camera in his hand pass by the window. I nodded at the usher I had posted by that door who quickly exited the worship center and outside of my gaze, guided the cameraman and reporter with him outside.

I went on.

"Now, unfortunately, when someone who claims to be religious (or in our case, a follower of Christ), and that person is angry and judgmental toward sin, it communicates that, perhaps, God is that way too. People reason, 'God's people are angry and judgmental toward sinners, so God must be that way as well.' It's not true. The Scripture says otherwise, but that is the way people think just the same."

"There is another reason that people think God is angry and judgmental, and it has nothing to do with God or other people and the way they are. Instead, it has everything to do with us."

"Have you ever wondered...*if the Bible says, 'God is love,' then why do people fear Him?* The answer is simple. It is because of their sin. The Bible tells us in Isaiah 59 that our sin cuts us off from God. You see it's our sin that alienates us from Him. But our sinful condition also causes us to play the blame game. But we don't blame ourselves for the alienation we feel between Him and us. We blame God. We assume that He is the one who caused the separation. He must be angry with us. So, we begin to fear Him."

"It's kind of like the little boy who does something wrong and is scolded by his parents. So, he puffs out his lower lip and says, 'You hate me.' Of course, we all know it's not true. They don't hate their little boy."

"And when our transgressions cause a separation between us and God, we also think He hates us. But He doesn't any more than Mom and Dad hate their little son. God's love for us remains intact no matter what we've done and no matter what we feel."

About this time, I looked up and through the glass strip in the rear doors to our auditorium I saw Raymond and Sarah standing outside the worship center. They were waiting for the right moment to come in and my wife was with them. I knew they wanted to slip in unnoticed and wait near the back until it was their turn to stand before the church. I looked toward the back of the auditorium and the two chairs we had ready for them were in place and empty, the only empty chairs in the auditorium.

Having compiled all this in my mind in just a moment, I continued.

"Our God is one of mercy and love. If He gave us what we deserved at midnight tonight, we would never see a minute of tomorrow and beyond. But He doesn't. That's why God's love for us is the best news in the universe."

"Verse 35 asks, 'Who shall separate us from the love of Christ?' However, it really isn't asking a question as much as it is making a statement. And that statement is this: 'God's love is big and vast;' yet, it is not talking about size."

"We have sung songs growing up in the church all our lives that say, 'God's love is as big as an ocean.' But this verse is not referring to how large God's love is. It is talking about scope. It is talking about the capabilities and the character of His love."

"First, the scripture says, 'God's love is so big trouble will not separate us from it.' It is saying when we have calamity—when we have bad things happen to us, or when we are without food or money—does that mean God doesn't love us anymore? Does it mean He has deserted us? The Bible says emphatically...*No. Absolutely not!* None of those things are indications that God doesn't love us anymore, because God's love is much bigger in character than that."

I looked out over the church and I could see people were beginning to wipe their eyes. It surprised me, because I didn't expect, if tears were going to flow, they would flow only when Raymond stepped up to talk. And, I wasn't sure the tears would be anyone else's other than Raymond's.

I also glanced over at the door and saw through the window that Raymond and Sarah were still standing outside, apparently reluctant to enter and draw attention to themselves.

I went on.

"Then why do these things happen? Well, sometimes trouble naturally follows sin. Sometimes stuff just happens. But none of it means that God's love for us has come to an end. In 1 Timothy 1:13, Paul tells of the awful attitude he had, before he was a Christian, toward Christ, the church, Christianity, and the God of Christianity. He said, *'I was formerly a blasphemer, a persecutor, and an insolent man.'* He claimed he was the worst of all sinners. Yet, Paul said that God's love and mercy was extended to him."

"Well, if Paul is the worst and God's love and mercy was extended to him, then certainly it would be extended to us, too.

When I was in high school, I was made leader of my church youth group. But when I went to school and was with my friends, with my actions I would deny God. I would speak unholy words, join in sinful conversations and discussions, and would do things I knew were wrong. Why…because I was ashamed of God. I wanted people's approval rather than God's approval. I wanted it even though I was a leader in my church youth group. This created terrible guilt in my heart. I was living a lie. And deep down, I thought, *God has surely cut me off now.* But when I truly surrendered my heart to Him, figuratively, I turned and looked into His face. When I did, I found that He was right there waiting for me with His arms wide open. He was ready to embrace me and welcome me into His family, even though in my mind, I had done something that was unforgivable. God's love for us just doesn't end."

Glancing toward the back again I could see that Raymond and Sarah were still standing in the hall continuing to postpone their entrance. But as I was about to proceed, in a quick burst, they walked through the door and briskly scurried to the two open seats we reserved for them.

When they sat down, there was an undercurrent of mumbles, whispers, and movement. A few people leaned to the side or rose to move and pat them on their shoulders. Then the air quieted again.

I glanced around quickly to see how the Gil's entrance had affected the rest of the audience, but all seemed fine, and people were intent to hear what else I had to say. Maybe it was because people sensed my message was leading up to an important revelation or announcement of some kind about the events of the previous two days. Perhaps they thought they would hear from the Gils themselves. I wasn't sure, but whatever the case, it was obvious people were very focused on the words coming from the pulpit that morning.

I continued with my sermon, expounding on Romans as I felt God had directed me for the next several minutes. As I did, I could detect an ever-increasing sense of God's presence with us. At a certain point, the whites of tissues and handkerchiefs could be seen throughout the auditorium; and I could hear sniffles and see tears.

Raymond, no doubt occupied by his upcoming confession and his shame, kept his head bowed the entire time. Sarah looked straight ahead—not at me as I talked—just straight ahead. I, on the other hand, was moved to the depth of my soul, overcome by the previous week, the death of Christina, and the sense of grace that seemed to be filling the whole place.

When I finished, I looked around. Except for a periodic cough, the room was filled with spellbinding silence. The sniffles had stopped, and the tissues were gone. As I surveyed the auditorium, I actually *felt* the Bible verse, *"Be still, and know that I am God"* (Psalm 46:10). For a few moments, I didn't dare speak. The quietness was too sacred to disturb with my feeble words. So, I stood there motionless and silent for several seconds.

CONFESSIONS

Finally, quietly, but deliberately, I spoke. I informed the people concerning the content of what was about to be discussed and that there was a good possibility it *wasn't* going to be G-rated. I wanted to be sure if young ears were present, parents had opportunity to take their children out of the service.

Next, I said, "That which is about to take place is family business. If you are a visitor, I am not going to ask you to leave. You may stay if you want. But if you feel uncomfortable to do so, you may leave at this time."

I also addressed any possible media who may have slipped by our security. I said, "If there is anyone here who is from the media, television stations, newspapers or magazines, I humbly ask that you leave at this time. If you stay, we don't give permission for you to report anything you observe from this service."

When all noise and movement came to a stop, I introduced Raymond by saying, "There is a lot of talk and speculation about the events surrounding the death of Christina Gil, and God has laid it upon the heart of Raymond to come and share with you."

Then I said, "Raymond and Sarah, would you come now?"

It took a few minutes for the two of them to get in position. While they were doing so, I said, "What Raymond is going to talk to you about today was not something we desired from him. He asked me if he could do this. So, at Raymond's request our church leadership is permitting him to speak to us today."

Raymond was red-eyed and feeble as he stepped up to the podium and placed a single sheet of paper on the stand. I glanced over at Sarah. She was standing behind Raymond and next to my wife, who was beside her for support. Raymond stood with body hunched and head down.

Sarah's posture was nothing of the kind. She stood tall, proper, and statue-like with a look of prideful formality on her face. I knew it wasn't pride she felt though, nor formality. Sarah was living out the shock she entered into over a week before. It had tapered off about Wednesday or Thursday but was reinstated with multiplied intensity when Christina was murdered. Now Sarah was standing before her church family at the peak of her trauma. What Raymond *did* was shameful, but what Sarah *felt* was shame. But she stood there nonetheless, in shock, in shame, but proper and formal; and yet, in support of her husband.

I glanced back at Raymond as he broke the silence with his first words.

"I need to tell you what has happened in the last few weeks that caused my daughter's death," he began in his gruff voice. Since he had been crying, his words sounded even coarser, as if he was fighting off a lingering case of laryngitis.

"I'm not proud of what's happened," he continued tearfully. "I . . . I . . . I'm not totally the person you think I am. I love my wife and my daughter." With tears representing pain and shame now filling his words, he said, "I would do anything for them. But what I've done in the past few weeks has caused my daughter's death."

Raymond never looked up. With his head still down, he just took a deep breath, and another, and another. When he could go on, he said . . .

"I need to tell you that in the past few years, I've questioned where I was sexually. And . . . uh . . . every once in a while, I would go to adult bookstores. At one of these visits about two months ago, I met Dan . . . we hit it off right away."

Out of the corner of my eye, I looked over at Sarah. She was still standing tall and formal. It seemed to me that she looked proper, but inside she was holding back the scream of her life. She didn't scream though, and she didn't break character.

Raymond, slowly and still seeming to be nursing a constricted throat, kept on . . .

"He seemed to be a very nice person . . . a very funny person. We enjoyed doing things together. We enjoyed talking. We'd go to the rec center. We'd go to eat. He didn't have a job, so he came to our city and started working for me. He would take the bus here."

I was a bit uncomfortable with all Raymond's talk about his relationship with Daniel, and I looked out over the crowd to see how they were responding. I didn't see any looks of disapproval, only sympathy. So, I turned back toward Raymond as he continued.

"Then I would take him back to the stop and he'd take the bus back to where he lived. A few times I would take him back home myself and I'd stay with him, coming back in the evening. Eventually he insisted that I come to pick him up everyday. After he moved here, I had to assist him with his apartment, and that's when we became really close."

Raymond paused, and then said with his head way down,

"We did some things that I'm not proud of."

Then Raymond took a deep breath and went on.

"After a while he started insisting that he was in love with me. When we worked, he would not let me do anything.

He said, 'I can't let you do that. I love you too much.' And he would do all the heavy work. Then he started insisting that I move in with him. I knew I shouldn't, but in some respect, I apparently led him on."

"He held on to me by saying, 'If you leave, I will tell everybody what we have been doing, and I will add things to it.' He said, 'I will embellish it.'"

"I told him, 'Those embellishments aren't true.'"

"And he said, 'The people will believe it...it doesn't matter what you say. The people will believe me.'"

"He wanted to be with me all the time. Sometimes we'd go to the rec center, and it would be nine o'clock at night before I would get home. Last week, he pushed really hard for me to come and live with him, and I said, 'I can't.'"

"He said, 'If you don't do it now, I'll go and tell your wife and you'll have to come.' So last Saturday night, he forced me to tell my wife that I was leaving her; and I left her and went to live with him."

It was at this time I looked over the audience and for the first time I saw *beauty*. I have had plenty of dealings with people who don't walk in a faith relationship with Jesus Christ. I've seen the way they respond to people with tales less harrowing than Raymond's. Their response is largely skepticism. Moreover, their attitudes are untrusting, angry, blaming, and intolerant. But as I looked into the faces of people listening to Raymond, I saw compassion. Not one person that I could see had that squinted-eye or gritted-teeth look. And I didn't see sympathy; I saw empathy. I saw a look on people's faces that said, "Raymond, I'm not weeping for you. I'm weeping with you." It was my first real glimpse of the church's *beauty*.

Raymond hadn't pulled a fast one on them. He is not a stupid man, but he isn't clever enough to mislead them and get away with it. I'm not sure anyone in a circumstance like this could be that clever. No, Raymond had been broken. The people in our church that day had sensed it, and there was an interchange of brokenness and pardon happening that was genuine and absolutely beautiful, and Raymond wasn't even aware of it. He was too overcome by his objective of confessing his faults to be able to see it. So, Raymond just kept talking.

Sarah wasn't aware of it either. She was too overcome by shock and shame to be able to detect something so tender. She continued to stand straight and proper.

My observation of this *beauty* caused me to begin to weep and lightly shake in awe of the moment and anticipation of what God was going to do. I wondered if anyone noticed I was shaking, and I took a deep breath to try and calm myself.

Raymond plodded on . . .

"Dan was with me constantly. He wouldn't leave me alone. I couldn't call. He monitored my cell phone calls. He monitored all of them. He wouldn't let me talk to Sarah. The only person he let me talk to was Christina. I didn't know how to get out of it. I didn't know what to do."

"At the dentist's office, he sat in the lobby and waited for me to make sure I didn't do anything I shouldn't. I was able to sneak away and make a couple of phone calls to Sarah, not knowing Sarah and Chris were working together to do something."

Raymond did *not* become more comfortable as he talked. He may have glanced up periodically to appear engaged, but largely he kept his eyes and face glued to the podium or down toward the floor. It didn't appear he was reading. Apparently, the humiliation he felt was prohibiting him from making eye contact with anyone.

I've heard of individuals telling their nervous child or a friend giving a speech to keep his or her eyes on them for moral support, because they will be watching enthusiastically, and it will give the speaker confidence. But Raymond, at least in his own mind, had no one to look at in the whole wide world. No one would be sitting in the audience with the sole intention of giving Raymond moral support. So, he kept his head aimed downward for the entire time. Raymond was crying rather freely by this time, and it was getting more difficult to understand what he was saying. But he continued telling the story, though he was slurring his words with regularity now.

With his head down, Raymond went on . . .

"On Thursday night, the police came to the apartment, took me outside, and asked, 'Do you really want to be here?'"

"I started crying and I told the officer that I didn't want to be there." He said, 'Go in and pack your things and leave. We'll keep Dan away from you.' I did what he requested and went back to the church where Chris, Shirley and Sarah were waiting for me. I was so happy. Christina was so happy when I came home. We decided not to stay at the house, and we stayed at a hotel that night."

"The next morning, Daniel called me on my cell phone and said everything was OK; that he was going back east to live with his parents...that I didn't have anything to worry about. Sarah and I went down to the courthouse and proceeded with some restraining orders against him. By the time I finished at the courthouse, my daughter was dead."

At this point, Raymond couldn't continue with both tears and talk. He just stood there and cried, not loudly...just whimpering. I wanted to go and put my arm around his shoulder, but something said, *"No...Raymond needs to stand alone before these people."*

Again, I looked at the crowd as Raymond stood before them weeping. I could detect something of divine presence settling over all of us. Yes, there were people crying, and it was hard not to feel sorry for Raymond as he stood there in pain. But it wasn't sympathy or even empathy I sensed right then. I was sensing a holy kind of *God-likeness* descending upon the crowd. It almost seemed as if it wasn't about Raymond or Sarah or Daniel or Christina or any other human for that matter. It was now becoming about God.

Finally, after several moments, Raymond managed some more words to conclude his weepy confession, unaware of the divine aura present. He said . . .

"And . . . and . . . and my world has been torn apart. What Dan said has come true. He has totally hurt me. I'm so ashamed for what I've done. I've hurt my family. I've helped kill my daughter."

And with one last surge of strength, through sobs and pain, Raymond concluded . . .

"And I hope that God can forgive me for what I've done."

To say there wasn't a dry eye in the place would do the moment a great injustice. Yes, people were crying...me included. But it seemed the God who made us all was the one weeping; and He was doing so through the tears of those present that morning. It was more than just that people were crying for Raymond, Sarah, and Christina. It seemed the people in our little church that fateful morning were crying for the whole plight of pain on Earth, the kind of pain God feels when He considers the evil and suffering in the world. I couldn't explain it. I could only feel it.

Raymond stepped back from the lectern, and with his head down, motioned for me to take over as he choked out, "OK...OK."

BEAUTY

I could hardly speak myself. I stepped forward to the podium and stood there before speaking long enough to be sure my words could be understood through my tears. Then I choked out these few short sentences.

> "God's forgiveness is a given. But how do we feel about what we just heard? Can we forgive Raymond? If you can forgive Raymond, would you come up here and embrace him?"

That is all I could get out. I had planned to say something different and more, but those were the words that came from my lips. After I spoke, I stepped back and I watched as I wiped the moisture from my eyes.

I remember thinking, *I have never seen a moment in ministry like this, where the atmosphere was so broken, so humble, so beautiful.*

Raymond was so incredibly broken; he could have crumbled into a heap of bones at any moment, both physically and spiritually.

But the environment of the entire room was broken as well. I could feel the hearts of people broken for Raymond, but they were also broken of pride. People were being challenged to forgive, not just by the pastor, but also by the Holy Spirit. The whole place felt humble, and as a result; clean, holy, pure, and hallow. We were on *holy ground*. All that was missing was a burning bush.

The atmosphere was simply draped in humility. People's hearts, from Raymond to the most obscure person in the back of the room—were broken, pliable, and moldable for God's purposes. And the very air felt clean; not like rain had fallen to rid the air of dust. It was like spiritual rain had fallen from heaven and had cleansed every heart and soul, leaving them spotless before God and man. It was beautiful. I wasn't sure how many others felt it, but I did. Nor was I aware of it then, but soon I would learn what was giving rise to the purified atmosphere I sensed.

After I had given the people my charge, in spite of the things I felt, no one moved. People seemed frozen to their seats. As I looked out over the room, I wondered *had I read it wrong? Were people really disgusted with Raymond and the truth of their disgust was now being revealed?* It seemed like an eternity before anyone stirred.

Eventually, one man stood and walked slowly toward the front. He stepped onto the platform and up to Raymond. He stood there with his arms hanging at his side and looking at Raymond long enough for me to wonder...*is he going to hug him or slap him?* Finally, the man reached out both his arms and gathered them around Raymond. Into Raymond's ear, in a low voice only loud enough for those of us on the platform to hear, he said, "Raymond, I forgive you."

Raymond said nothing. No words would come. He just sobbed in the man's arms. Then the man released Raymond, walked over to Sarah, took both of her hands in his, and said, "We love you and we support you."

Sarah continued to stand tall and formal. She smiled properly and thanked him as he moved to the side and off the platform.

I was so enthralled with this first individual that I didn't see the second until he was already standing in front of Raymond. He too embraced the broken man and whispered his forgiveness into Raymond's ear as Raymond just sobbed. Then he released him and moved to the side to offer his support to Sarah.

I looked up and there was a third, and then a fourth. One-by-one, men and women left their seats and walked silently onto the stage to embrace this shattered family and offer to them their support and forgiveness. Music was being played to fill the air with comfort, but it seemed to be almost undetectable, because the very nature of God expressed through His love and forgiveness was being manifested in and through the hearts of His people. And that morning, *His nature* was making *its* own kind of music. It was filling the air with holiness, and it was beautiful. It was pure. It was clean. It was God's presence there in church in a way I had never seen before. It was a moment in His presence I wished would never end.

So prevalent was God's presence there, people knew not to speak or discuss what was happening, as if human words would desecrate the sacredness they felt.

I looked over the crowd again. The pattern of one-by-one was still in place, each one giving individual and genuine forgiveness and support to Raymond and Sarah. And Raymond never stopped crying.

I looked to the back of the auditorium and each person, after their offering to the Gils, rather than leave, went to the back of the room and formed a random crowd standing across the rear of the building. It seemed everyone knew they weren't to leave until all had expressed their forgiveness to Raymond. To leave would have compromised the solidarity of support people instinctively knew they should give to this broken family.

I looked back toward the front, near where Raymond was standing on the platform and where people were still moving one at a time toward him.

And I noticed something else.

I saw people stepping up to Raymond and looking him in the eye but wanting the broken man to look back at them in the same way, because his head was hung in shame.

It reminded me of the scripture in Psalms 3:3, *"But you, O Lord, are a shield for me, my glory and the One who lifts up my head."*

In this case, God was using the compassionate hearts in His church to demonstrate His restorative heart. God is the glory and the lifter of our heads from shame, guilt, condemnation, and sin. But God wanted Raymond to see that the very ones he feared would reject him, would instead, graciously forgive, love, and accept him for a far more grievous transgression—one that had bearing on the death of his daughter. God's very nature of love and forgiveness being manifested in and through their hearts toward Raymond was lifting Raymond's head from shame to acceptance, from guilt to forgiveness, from sin to salvation.

I was amazed, but not at the interaction of confession and acceptance between a man and a group of people. I was amazed at the *beauty* of Christ's bride.

I knew well the scriptures that painted the church as the bride of Christ. Though I had read and even studied them, I had never actually interpreted the actions of the church as being beautiful before. I thought perhaps the Scripture was using the bride analogy to describe the way Jesus felt about His church. Or, I felt it referred to the beauty of His church draped in the spotless white garments of holiness because of Christ's perfect sacrifice on the cross, but not from anything they had done. Or, in my mind I thought, maybe it stood for the way the church would appear one day in the presence of God. But never had I interpreted any of it to mean the church of Jesus Christ, His body and His bride, could perform glorious acts of beauty right here on planet Earth—until this day.

I had seen the bumper sticker that read, "Perform Senseless Acts of Beauty and Random Acts of Kindness." But that day, I witnessed *acts of beauty* that weren't at all senseless. They were filled with mindful, logical, purposeful moral richness and genuineness, the likes of which I had never beheld.

As I watched the people pardon Raymond and love Sarah, I was sure the *beauty* I was beholding was related to forgiveness. As God had forgiven, people were now forgiving. They were doing so one-by-one, person-by-person, saint-by-saint. This brought another thought to my mind.

It seemed each person; man or woman, boy or girl was deciding individually to forgive Raymond. I never saw a flood of people move to the front in mass. Each seemed to move as God impressed him or her to forgive. And I thought that's *it*. That is the *beauty* of the church: God's forgiveness of us, demonstrated by Him on a cross, and then lived out by His Church to undeserving sinners.

And I thought, *People who don't know God don't know or see this beauty. They are more apt to see revenge, hatred, bitterness, unforgiveness, strife, backbiting, blackballing, and loathing. Most of the world has no concept of the loveliness of the love of God. I thought…if they could only be here today. What a sight they would behold!*

Stepping forward I said . . .

"Thank you for the overwhelming show of your love, forgiveness, and support for Raymond and Sarah. You've helped them to face the future with a greater sense of hope and acceptance."

"At Raymond's request, he and Sarah would like to slip out without talking with anyone. This was an emotional time for them, and more interaction would be draining for them."

The people understood.

With that, I had our elders and leadership come forward. The people were still lined up all around the worship center walls several bodies thick. As one we all prayed for and over Raymond and Sarah. We then allowed them to move out of the room, down the hall, and out the back door of the church to their waiting automobile.

For as long as I have been in the ministry, whenever I have preached a message that has been especially delivered from my heart, and when I have felt great emotional conviction about what I have just said, it is difficult for me to interact with people immediately afterward. Often, I will talk blank-faced to people, until I sense an opportunity to break away. Then I will retreat to my office to think in order to seal the moment in my heart and with the Lord. I hadn't felt that way about my message necessarily, but I felt more that way than ever before about the whole experience I had just beheld.

The demeanor of the people that day after the service was quiet anyway, and once the Gils left, people just seemed to want to offer their good-byes and go home. So, everyone silently exited the building rather quickly and left the property.

As the crowd thinned out, I slipped into my office. Entering and before the door closed, I burst into tears for a fourth time in the same amount of days. But it wasn't pain for the Gils I was feeling. I had a sense something bigger, something more related to God's purposes, had been going on that day.

While in my office, I spoke to the Lord through my tears, *Lord, I don't understand how You work. I don't understand Your sovereignty or Your omniscience, but I am in awe of You. I am in awe of how You could take something so ugly, so grotesque, so hideous, and make it so beautiful.*

I wasn't sure at that time what good the *beauty* of that event would accomplish beyond the event itself. But I was certainly basking in the moment of God's glory. Who would have thought a crisis so devastating could emerge so glorious?

I found myself there in my office losing sight, even if just for a moment, of the pain Raymond and Sarah were submerged in. It wasn't because I didn't care, but because I was convinced by then that the whole event was no longer about them. Nor was it about Daniel's sin or the evil in the world, or our church, or my ministry. It was now about God and His purposes. I wasn't sure why I felt it; I just did. What I didn't know was exactly what those purposes were.

In just a little over a week's time, we had been on an incredible journey. It was a journey that started with us stepping into hell. From there, we traveled to the deepest, darkest recesses of the nether world. And I wasn't sure how it happened, but somehow, on the morning of Day Nine, we had emerged in heaven. This could not have been accomplished through anything of my own doing, nor the Gils, nor our church. It was, purely and simply; a wonder only God could have accomplished.

I packed up and went out into the foyer of the church in time to see my wife come around a corner.

"We're the last ones here again," she said.

I responded, "Then let's go home."

That was Day Nine…the most beautiful day I have ever beheld in the ministry.

EVERY DAY SINCE

The first-degree murder conviction of Daniel Rogers was short and sweet—bittersweet. The trial didn't take place until many months after Christina's murder. But when it finally did, it took the twelve-person jury just forty-five minutes to find him guilty of murder in the first degree. He managed to escape the death penalty because the District Attorney was unwilling to call Daniel's case a *capital* murder case. But he sits in a cell in fear of his life every day because of the disdain prisoners feel toward their peers who kill children. Christina was an adult, but still a teenager.

About four weeks before Christina's death, my wife had a prayer time with God. She was actually whining.

We began as pastors of the church where the Gils attended some years before Christina's death had taken place; and it was a struggle right from the beginning. It seemed as if time after time we had been attacked by perils beyond our control; perils having to do with finances, our family, the church, and just life. It was as if every time we took one step forward, something would happen to force us back two.

As Shirley was praying that day in mid August about a month before the fateful day, she asked the Lord a one-word question, "When?" In other words, *Lord, when are You going to begin to do something in our church?*

She wasn't really soliciting an answer from God as much as she was just crying out to Him; sort of lamenting about all the hardships we had been through since we came to the church. To be more frank, she was complaining; actually, expressing both hers and my frustration with our church's inability to make a significant impact for God in our city.

To her surprise, she sensed a response from God, which He revealed to her mind. It wasn't an audible voice she heard. It was more a sense, a kind of awareness; and she was certain it was from the Lord.

She felt God impress upon her this answer. "...A little while longer."

If anyone in our family hears from the Lord, it is Shirley. We aren't people who see God's face in shadows or on light bulbs. We don't walk in la-la land concerning the leading of the Lord. There have been only a few times in our lives when we have sensed God's strong leading, and for Shirley, this was one of them.

Being the impetuous one she is; my wife couldn't merely wait on God for His interpretation of what "a little while longer" meant. So, the next day she prayed again, but this time she stepped out on a limb of presumption and boldly said...*Lord, I am certain You spoke to me yesterday and told me we would have to wait for things to begin to happen in our church "a little while longer."* Then she asked...*Lord, could You tell me how much longer?*

She had no sooner asked this question, but in her mind, she heard an answer, one that seemed very unusual; yet one she felt certain was also from the Lord. She heard God say, "*Thirty days.*"

My wife's first reaction was . . . *Thirty days! Did I hear that right? Did I make that up in my mind or did God actually say that to me?* She decided . . . *No, I couldn't have made it up. It was too unusual of a response, too clearly spoken and heard, too impossible a task for anyone but God to perform. It could not have been my imagination.*

Shirley wrote the date on her calendar. Then she turned the page over to September and marked an X on the day that was exactly a month from the day she heard God speak.

That weekend, Shirley told me about her encounter with the Lord and His two answers: "A little while longer," and, "Thirty days." She also told me about the September date just to be accountable, which I put on my calendar as well.

We prayed together to seal the promise, and oddly, both of us forgot all about it. How could someone so easily forget about something so precise, so extraordinary, so bizarre?

I guess, in the natural, the occupation of our time must have been the reason for our absentmindedness. The last part of August and the first few weeks of September is always a busy time for church work. It is when new programs and schedules typically get under way. Meetings with ushers, teachers, leaders, and staff seem to bottleneck into this time of the year. We must have become caught up in the bustle of getting ministry-business done.

Or maybe God had something to do with our lapses in memory. But on that September day, the day of Christina's murder, both of us were jolted back into recollection, for that was the thirtieth day.

For me, this realization came to me while I was on the way to the department store with the Gils. Raymond and Sarah were in the car with me and in mortal terror concerning the wellbeing of their daughter. As we drove, I glanced at my watch and saw the day God gave to Shirley on the date display. That is when it hit me.

My God, No! Is this what you meant Lord, when you spoke to Shirley? I shouted in my thoughts. My mouth fell wide open in awe as I pondered the possibility, and of course I said nothing to Raymond and Sarah. But I was stunned. I can still see the place where that realization dawned on me.

There have been only a few times in my life when a significant event took place and my location at the time of its occurrence was stamped indelibly into my mind. Some of mine are perhaps the same as yours: President Kennedy's assassination, the Challenger disaster, and 9/11. My fourth, I'm sure, was mine and mine alone; the realization that God had indirectly predicted Christina's death; and that it had something to do with what was going to happen in the church.

From that location to the store, which was perhaps five blocks from the spot, I was in my own kind of shock. Of course, I laid it aside amid all the confusion that followed.

For my wife the same realization also came to her while she was in her car. I had called her by cell phone when I was on the way to the police department from Christina's store. I called to tell her the awful news and to ask her to come to the station to be with Sarah. Shirley immediately jumped into her car and headed for the police station.

As she was ready to turn the corner onto the street where the police station was located, the same epiphany hit Shirley. She too realized, *My God! This is "The Day;" the day God said would be significant in our lives and church.* She was so overwhelmed as this awareness came to her, she had to pull the car over to collect herself. She sat there in her own place of shock for several moments before she could even drive again.

But here is where this part of the story gets bizarre.

The routes from the Gil home to the department store where Christina worked (the route I took); and the route from the church to the police station, (the one my wife took); for a time overlap each other. The spots where *"The Day"* dawned on me—and where it dawned on Shirley—were identical.

I am not superstitious, but I do believe in a sovereign God who is able to manipulate time and space for His purposes. It happened time and time again in the Bible. It can—and does—happen today. It wasn't until later that evening that we would be able to compare notes and report our discoveries to each other.

Why God would have choreographed an identical epiphany location for us, I don't know; unless it was simply that He wanted to make certain we were unmistakably convinced of His involvement in this event. It did indeed convince us.

With the knowledge that God was up to something, albeit something far too above me to comprehend, I attempted to cooperate with what I assumed must have been God's intent to reach many people in our city.

I put numerous hours into Christina's funeral and the events surrounding it, which took place the Thursday following her death. I attended vigils and candle light services at the department store and Christina's grave, where dozens of her friends and workmates gathered to remember her. I also tried to keep up my relationship with several people who knew Christina to perhaps, influence them to come to Christ.

When the time for the trial came up the following year, I stepped up my efforts to reach people as well; still feeling God had intent to use the tragedy of Christina's death to reach large numbers of people. I was absolutely amazed concerning all of it: that an event such as *this one* could ever happen in the church; that I would ever be so close to something that inconceivable; and that God would sovereignly use an incident such as this to reach people.

Yet, as much as I thought God's intent in all of it was to draw many in our city to Him; and as hard as I tried to act in concert with it, very little happened. At the funeral a few people acknowledged their need for a closer walk with Jesus, and that was good.

Largely, however, we saw very few results from our efforts. And since that was the case, it was always a mystery to me just what the event was all about; what God's answers to my wife's prayers were about; and what Christina's death on that fateful September day was all about.

For a while, I thought I was supposed to write a book about it, but I never felt good about any of the ideas I had for the storyline. I am also someone who has great difficulty writing about anything unless it can at least conclude with good news. And up until that time I wasn't sure that the Gil-marriage would end that way. Eventually I let the idea of a book die.

A few years later, Shirley and I resigned as pastors of that church, feeling that our time was finished there. Once we resigned, it escalated my uncertainty regarding what God's purpose had been for us there.

I was even more confused when the Gil's relationship began to falter. They went to a professional Christian counselor for more than a year. For a time, they faithfully prayed and read the Bible together each morning. Sarah's shock took some time to wear off, but when it did, what emerged was a great deal of pent-up anger in her heart for her husband. She weathered it as much as she could, but soon Raymond's critical tendencies returned, and along with them, other inclinations.

At a certain point Sarah separated and filed for divorce. Today they live in different states. That ended my hope for the good news of a reconciled relationship for the Gils. And, as odd as it may seem, I could only see the story, as well as our pastorate there having real meaning, if there was a happy ending for Raymond and Sarah. I was somewhat stuck in that thinking. Consequently, I remained uncertain about the incident and what our time there was all about.

Then, one night in September, the same time of the year that the crisis occurred, and three years after Christina's death; I was awakened at three o'clock in the morning.

It was at precisely three in the morning that I woke up. It wasn't about three, or around three. When I opened my eyes and looked at my bedside clock, it read 3:00AM.

Three AM was the time that I had asked the Lord years earlier, "If you want to say anything to me at night, please say it at three in the morning so I know it is from you. It was the exact time I woke up with a call to the ministry in my heart. I have heard Him say other things to me as well when

I woke up at precisely 3:00AM confirming He was willing to take me up on my request.

This particular night in September, I woke up at exactly that time again, but this time with words in my mouth simultaneous with my waking up. I woke saying them as if it was a continuation of whatever I was dreaming…but I hadn't been dreaming. And I was saying them in a passionately argumentative tone to the Lord.

Those angst-filled words in the form of questions were, "What was our ministry in that city all about? Lord why did you send us there if we would not see anything significant happen? And what was Christina's murder all about? Lord, I don't understand; why did that happen?"

No sooner had I asked that final question, but I heard God say deep within my being, "It happened because you are supposed to write about it." Then, immediately following these words, in my mind, was the format for how it should be written; Day One, Day Two, and so forth. That is why Murder in the Church was written.

Now, instantly I knew God wasn't saying He had caused Christina's death so I could write a book, though the order of God's words may sound that way. God knew who He was talking to, and, knew that I knew better. I was fully aware that it was more like God was saying, "*It happened. Now your purpose is to write about it so that God can be glorified*" (John 9:1-3).

Then, to add to the marvel of His mandate to me that night, in the same moment I sensed I was to write the book, I recalled the glory of the service on Day Nine and I remember thinking…*Why didn't I see that before?*

The only explanations I have for not being able to recall the beauty of such an unbelievable service was; *first*, I was still traumatized from Christina's murder that had taken place only two days earlier. So, I was unable to see it as something glorious in those mortifying moments. And *second*, I wasn't supposed to see it until God was ready for me to write it. I think, since I was so focused on needing to see the good news of Raymond's and Sarah's marriage being saved; the possible reconciliation between them needed to be dead and gone for me to see the good news that was unveiled in the service on Day Nine.

That is the good news God wanted the world to see; *the forgiveness of God as seen in the forgiveness of his people.*

On that September Sunday, those in a gathering of people from His church experienced a heart-stopping glimpse of the *beauty* of The Church, a Church without spot or wrinkle (Ephesians 5:27), a Church as beautiful as a bride adorned for her husband (Revelation 21:2, 9), a Church reflecting the glory of the God of lights in whom there is no darkness at all (1John 1:5), only brightness, and glory, and beauty.

Every day since that one, I have been about declaring the *beauty* of His Church.

DAILY LESSONS

At a certain point in this story you may have entertained the thought...*I'm not sure I have the courage to continue.* As I have described certain aspects of the story to some that was their response, 'please stop, it is too sad', or 'too violent' or "too disturbing". But it will take true courage for you to plunge into this section of the book because lessons are hard to receive and even harder to implement into our lives. I challenge you to go one step further. If the story entertained you, this section may change you.

1) MARRIAGE

This is the first lesson I would like to address. In the story the key issue was an increasing air of *coldness* that developed between Raymond and Sarah. It could be seen in the story, but it is not uncommon in millions of marriages across our world.

Fighting Coldness. We have all observed older couples at restaurants sitting across from each other, staring into their food, or around the room, or at the waitress, or all the way through the physical images before them. But they never utter a word to each other throughout the entire meal other than to summon the bill or address a logistic. Not always, but often, it represents the age-old culprit against marital bliss . . . coldness.

We observed in the story (from hindsight mostly) the marks and some highly unusual consequences of a frozen marriage. We had several causes going on in the story, and in many marriages the same causes exist.

One cause of coldness is the *absence of nourishing and cherishing*. Ephesians 5:29 tells husbands to nourish and cherish their wives. Nourish means to feed, emotionally and spiritually. Cherish means to actively and physically encourage and appreciate.

Husbands can build strength into their marriages by simply nourishing their wives with love and tenderness. This kind of treatment from husbands to their wives can build respect and trust in their spouses that can become the building blocks of a strong and enduring relationship.

Husbands can further firm up the foundation and framework of their marriage by actively and physically showing appreciation for their wives. He can offer a love-look, a cherish-wink, an approving touch; to let his wife know how special and cherished she is to him. Cherishing also includes talk. Conversation is one of the researched needs of wives. A husband merely talking to his wife about the day, the family, the house, the birds; communicates to her that her man cherishes her enough to give his two most valuable possessions—his time and his heart.

Several years ago, friends gave us a porch swing. We hung it from our porch ceiling, and it has become in no uncertain terms, the glue that has held our marriage together. Mornings on days off, evenings after dinner, other times we have opportunity and sometimes when we don't; we gravitate to the swing to talk about anything and everything. When we moved to another city, we took it down and brought it with us to our new house. And it served us in our marriage in our new location. Great amounts of nourishing and cherishing through conversation have occurred there.

My advice is . . . *find your porch swing.* It may be a bench in a park, a boulder on a hillside or a pathway you may walk together. But whatever it is—find it.

When these actions are missing as they were in the marriage we observed in the story, the relationship is destined for coldness and other possible sinister evils.

Other causes of coldness are issues related to *empty nest syndrome.* An empty nest is a home where the children have moved out. Empty nests themselves do not cause coldness in marriage. However, the issues that create this syndrome in a marriage are symptoms of the condition.

Christina, though still living in the Gil house, was very absent. She had a boyfriend and many other close acquaintances and spent very little time at home. Raymond and Sarah were clearly on the verge of having an empty nest. Sarah, and especially Raymond, had paved the way for empty nest syndrome quite completely by redirecting the primary focus of their family love toward Christina rather than toward each other.

When a relationship between a husband and a wife becomes founded and reliant upon either or both of their relationships with their children; it stands to reason, when the children are gone, the marriage has little hope. Often, when the last child leaves, the father and mother turn and look at each other and wonder . . . *who is this stranger in my house?*

Husbands and wives need to do everything they can to keep their love alive as their children move through the adolescent developmental process; date nights, taking some vacations alone when the kids are older, finding common interests and so forth. As strange as it seems, it really is a healthier attitude when parents are pushing their kids out of the nest . . . rather than wishing they could keep them there forever.

Over-possessiveness at the time kids are ready to leave home at adulthood, may be a telltale sign that spouses are fearing what may occur between them when the kids are gone.

On the other hand, those parents who are more anxious to see their children leave may represent two people who aren't afraid to be *one on one* again. It appears to be a relationship that has kept love alive and vital, independent of their love for their children. This isn't only best for their relationship after the kids leave; it is also best for the kids while they are still in the home. It models a pattern of health in marriage for their children to feel safe in while they are still in the home. And it gives their children an example to follow once they are ready to form their own marriage and family.

The last cause of marital coldness seen in the story is *pornography*. The Bible's warning is against lust. In Matthew 5:28 Jesus says, *"But I say to you that whoever looks at a woman to lust for her has already committed adultery with her in his heart."* How much more controlling and destructive is the power of lust when a pictured piece of paper, or a disc, or a piece of film with another image of a sexual temptation on it, has taken one's heart captive. Marriages all over the world have crashed or are in trouble because of the power of pornography. Never mind whether it is a man or a woman on the images or doing the lusting. The Bible gives clear instruction concerning this; however, we will save that for another discussion later in this chapter. But faithfulness should never be in question. And since lust is the same as adultery in God's eyes, it should be clear as to the reason God warns against this sin.

Pornography causes married people to be unfaithful to their spouses. They are unfaithful just by looking at it, listening to it, reading it, or watching it on film. Continued unfaithfulness with pornography also causes love-loss resulting in coldness, alienation and separation. The argument that pornography saves marriages because it provides avoidance of an affair or prostitution is a weak one at best. Here's why. In God's Word Jesus says it is the same as adultery. And in normal marital situations, the victimized spouse feels as rejected and betrayed as if an affair has taken place.

Furthermore, pornography fills the participating partner's heart with fantasies about love and sex that are unrealistic and crippling to the intimacy between the marriage partners.

The extreme consequences observed in the story may never happen to most. However, similar results are seen all over our world in murders resulting from love triangles. You see them in the news and read about them in the papers daily. One should not dismiss the possibility of consequences such as these happening to him or her.

But the consequences of pornography are very real and very severe even if life-threat never enters the picture. Marriages are torn apart regularly because of constant indulgence with pornography by only one spouse. Don't be so foolish as to think that your relationship with your spouse won't pay a severe price because of your involvement with this destructive habit.

There are no exceptions. Pornography affects all related marital relationships in some adverse way. Many live in denial of these destructive consequences. But make no mistake about it. Your marriage relationship will suffer damaging results from dabbling with pornographic materials if you insist, and persist, in their usage.

At a time when several marriages were falling apart among pastors in the denomination I served, leaders suggested that each pastor go to see the movie "Fatal Attraction." It is a film about a man who is lured into a passionate one-night stand with an emotionally unstable woman he meets in his business dealings. After the affair he lets her down as gently as he can. But it was too late, and she was filled with resentment. The story ends with her stalking the unfaithful husband's family and attempting to murder him and his wife. The stalking woman is killed in self-defense and the story ends in relief. After pastor's watched the movie, some I talked with dismissed it as not affecting them greatly because the movie was fictional. The movie was fictional, but the scenario in the movie is as true as rain. These kinds of consequences do happen.

"But pornography is addicting," you say, "making it hard to stop." I have encountered men all over our country who have watched their marriages fritter away because they can't forgo this addictive pleasure. Indeed, it is nearly as addicting as drugs or alcohol. But its power is not from a foreign substance entering our bodies. Nor is it from a drug manipulating and confusing the pleasure centers of our brains.

This addiction is subject to the will alone. In Christ, there is certainly the power to say no to this temptation, the same as there is power to say no to a flirt from someone at your work or in your neighborhood, or to say no to a lie or performing an act of burglary. Stopping the power of pornography in our lives is as easy as saying no. Just consider the consequences, the alternatives, the wisdom in not succumbing, and the will of God; and saying no will become easier. And the more we say no, the easier the word is to form, and the more powerful our voicing of the word becomes.

How do you say No? Trash your magazines and videos. Talk to some one you can become accountable to. Eliminate the websites from your computer. Don't drive down the street the porn house is on any more. Cancel your subscriptions. Turn the TV off. Don't watch the cheerleaders at halftime anymore. Just say no.

Once a young man who had gone on a men's retreat over a weekend, came to me as his pastor and informed me that he had decided the previous weekend to stop his indulgence with pornography. He had talked to the speaker after a service and told him about his problem. The speaker told him to come to his pastor (who was of course me) when he arrived back home, bring his magazines to me, and together—burn them—all of them.

So, he did.

Together, we went out behind the church after a service, tore apart each book so each page would burn fully, and we torched them. The material in them, which was almost impossible for me to not see, was so disgusting; I felt I needed to repent just for catching a glimpse of it by accident. But the young man in coming to me had said . . . no. The act of going to all the trouble of engaging in a ceremony of victory, and with someone you respect and are accountable to; is a powerful way to say no. But, however you say no—say it!

2) PARENTING

The other day in the grocery store, in front of me I heard a lady spout angrily at her six-year-old boy (I presumed he was six) riding in her cart, "You're just stupid. Why do you say such God-d... stupid things?" I almost broke down in tears for the boy on the spot. And if I hadn't been so angry with the mother for saying such a thing to her son, I think I would have. I wanted to give her a tongue-lashing.

I told myself, *"Chris, this is none of your business."* But as I thought about it, I decided it was very much my business since the lady had abused her son right in front of me. But instead of scolding her, I leaned over the edge of the cart the boy was riding in and said loud enough for the mother to hear clearly, "Son, I just want you to know one thing. You are not stupid and don't *ever* let anyone tell you that you are."

The lady, pushing her cart before her, scurried away quickly, apparently ashamed. As the boy was being wheeled away, he leaned to the side of the cart, around the side of his mother's body and smiled at me; as if to say . . . *Thanks mister, I needed that, and so did my mom.*

Our human psyche is so fragile, even a perfect upbringing wouldn't create individuals with perfect self-images. But the fragility of our emotional make-ups should at very least, demonstrate the need for parents to handle their children's self esteem with kid gloves.

The jails are filled with children that grew up taken advantage of, or for granted, or abandoned, or abused, sexually, verbally, physically or emotionally, or all of the above. Many of these are tucked away from common folk in lifestyles that keep them in and out of the slammer.

But many more abused kids are very actively a part of our society—never entering jail—but spending their whole lives held up in their own private prisons of pain and dejection. Like dirty Linus in the Snoopy cartoons walks around emitting clouds of dust, many of these abused people we consider to be normal, walk around emitting disaster wherever they go. And our world is filled with them. They are our cousins, our brothers, our wives, husbands, mothers, fathers and children. Some of them . . . are you and me.

They emit disaster in their marriages. They emit disaster in their extended families. They emit disaster in their children's lives and families. They emit disaster at work. They emit disaster in every relationship they have. And it all started when Mom or Dad began tearing down their fragile self-esteem with remarks that would make a grown man cry . . . let alone a tender child.

God said he would, *"visit the sins of the fathers on the children to the third and fourth generations of those who hate Me"* (Exodus 20:5). That means simply, poor parenting will adversely affect families and family systems for years, even generations to come. And you can never predict just what evils may result from careless or intentionally destructive parenting.

In this story we saw the generational curse at work and an almost unbelievable result followed. However, in other cases, the curse may manifest itself in a host of other various and destructive ways.

Was Raymond's father as monster-like as Raymond described to me in the interviews he had with me in preparation for the writing of this book? It is hard to say. Maybe Raymond was exaggerating that some. However, if Raymond's father was half the brute Raymond described him to be, and as I described him in Day One of the story, he was still a severely abusive man and father.

Early on in my parenting responsibilities, I learned the power of parent's words and I chose and determined to never use certain words with my children. One obviously word was stupid, another idiot, another dumb, or the equivalent thereof.

The reality is, kids are uninformed and inexperienced in life and if they do or say something that suggests a lack of intelligence, it is almost always from a lack of information. They are too young to know the difference. However, it is our responsibility to teach them the difference. To call them stupid or its equivalent, for something they couldn't possibly know yet, is to contaminate the learning process. And sometimes parents call their kids stupid for something they learned to do while watching their parents. What is the irony in that?

But the real problem with abusive words like stupid, or dumb, or a myriad of other expressions careless parents use as they communicate with their children, is deep in the heart of the parent. All of us have hearts that are tainted with at very least, traces of anger, low self-esteem, hatred, resentment, jealousy, and a host of other sinful traits.

We are all capable of rattling off hurtful expressions in the stress of an emotional moment. Jesus said, *"Out of the abundance of the heart the mouth speaks"* (Matthew 12:34). But if our upbringings were less than exemplary, chances are the amounts of ugliness in our hearts are more than just traces. They may constitute bunches, or gobs, or in some cases mountains of ugliness. The more anger, hatred, jealousy, insecurity, etc. that is in a parent's heart—the more likely it is for that parent to be capable of vomiting their ugliness all over his or her children. And the more ugliness that is in a parent the more often and the more exaggerated their verbal abuse will be. The reality is; active volcanoes explode with increased regularity and intensity.

So, the source of parental abusive explosions is not the child's mistakes. It is the parent's heart. If you have a heart like this . . . seek counseling . . . quick!

The rule for correction when raising children is 10 to 1; that is, ten approving comments for every correcting comment. But even within this formula, never should we use a correcting remark in an abusive way or with abusive expressions.

So here is my point. Take God's advice on how to love and raise your children. In Ephesians 6:4 God says through Paul, *"Fathers, do not provoke your children to wrath, but bring them up in the training (some versions say nurture) of the Lord."* That means nurture them and guide them with God's love and tenderness.

To call a child stupid, or to treat him or her as though the child were of little worth, is to insert the power of evil, itself into the very soul of that little one. And there is no telling what kind of sinister results may come of it.

Parents, our society can't afford for us to fail in the child-rearing department. Every parent who fails makes our society worse. And that is to say nothing of the sorrows our failures bring to our own family systems for generations to come.

3) EMOTIONALLY DAMAGED

It is impossible to read down the list of abuses Raymond experienced at the hand of his father without feeling pity for him and his upbringing, but it's not a rare occurrence. Poor parenting is a stark reality on our culture today.

The bad news is; most who are abused don't know much beyond the blame they heap upon their parents. They spend their whole lives resenting one or both for the abuse and vowing to never let it happen in their family. They don't have any idea that they aren't right because of it and the way they behave has a direct connection to their upbringings. Furthermore, they never look within their own lives to see that they have experienced collateral damage. They don't realize they have been injured emotionally. More-so, they don't know that there is healing available in Christ.

We saw in the story that murder doesn't only happen to human bodies. It happens to human psyches.

However, in God there is . . . *repair*. Murdered psyches can be resurrected. It is possible, to a large degree, to repair the damage done to people from flawed upbringings.

Let's say a woman has walked her whole life under the weight of a poor self-concept from a less than adequate upbringing. That lady, as she comes to adulthood, can repair herself and improve the function-ability factors in her life. And men can do the same.

I look at the process as being similar to putting a square peg in a round hole. If a child is raised in a functional and healthy environment and manner; that child's life will fit into the systems of his or her existence as a round peg fits into a round hole. It may not fit perfectly because none of us are perfect, but it fits.

However, if a child is raised poorly in a poor environment, that child will have squared or rough edges in their lives reflecting their inability to fit into the emotionally stable systems around them. People go their whole lives trying to function in the normal systems of life, but because of the self-esteem deficit in their lives, they never really fit, and they never really function. This creates great stress and many destructive results. They fit into those lives like a square peg fits into a round hole.

But if one will first acknowledge and own his or her self-esteem challenges and the resulting dysfunctional issues in his or her life, and then seek counsel and accountability, that person can learn how to better function in this world. A counselor, whether a pastor or a professional therapist, may be able to help the person sand off the rough or squared edges of his or her life so he or she can fit better into the functional systems of this world. It will never be a perfect fit. But it can be a functional fit.

An account from my upbringing may serve as an example.

My father was an absentee dad. He wasn't around because he was always working, fishing, hunting, or involved in some other personally gratifying activity that kept him away from home and his family. When I played little league baseball, my father came to only one of my games. Just one . . . an All-Star game I was pitching in. But he never told me he was coming. He left before it was over, and he never talked to me about it afterwards; and never came to another. It is the only childhood activity of mine attended by my father until I was a sophomore in high school. My self-esteem suffered greatly from his lack of interest in me.

Later in his life he contracted emphysema, which landed him on disability; and he was forced to stay at home. When I began playing high school baseball, since my father was unable to go to work and was bored, he started to come to my ball games. Then suddenly he died. There was no opportunity to recoup from him the approval I had lost in my younger years.

Later in my life, I started to feel the effects of those early blights on my self-esteem. I found myself being very defensive about things that needed no defense. I found my self-confidence weak and my insecurity high. No beacon lights shone on these frailties revealing them to me. No red flags appeared over the issues in my life, so I knew they were problems needing to be dealt with. I just didn't like the way I felt. And I knew the issues in my adult life that were coming to the surface then, were tied to insecurities I had garnered from my childhood; and I knew they were not pleasing to the Lord.

Furthermore, I felt myself leading people as a pastor under the influence of the baggage I was carrying. It was nothing short of sheep abuse. In short, I was finding that I was not fitting very well into the normal and functional systems around me. Life was well rounded, but in my life, I had rough and squared edges . . . and I didn't fit. I had probably never fit very well. But I told myself I did and that I didn't have any emotional issues I needed to deal with. I was lying to myself, the same as many do about their issues.

When God got through to me about these things I went to a counselor, to start with. Then I made the issues in my life a matter of prayer. Every morning I would pray about the emotional deficiencies I sensed in my life. It was terribly humbling to own these personal frailties. But as I prayed about them, I sensed God building my self-assurance from the ground up (James. 4:10). Every day I would pray and every day I would feel stronger, not from having gained confidence in myself, but from having gained confidence in who I was becoming in God's strength.

I tell this entire story in another book I have written entitled "Once Broken." It is a book designed to assist people as they look to find emotional healing from the wounds of their past.

In Raymond's story and in his life, he never owned, or maybe even detected, some of his self-esteem issues. If he had, and had gone to a counselor at twenty-five or thirty, who knows? Perhaps he would have worked through some of the painful feelings he had for his father. Perhaps he would have never begun to question his sexual identity. Perhaps he would have been less prone to finding things wrong with his wife, his job, his church and his life.

But let me make an even more evident observation. The kind of admission I am talking about, especially for someone who has been raised in an environment, which all by itself, has intensified the pride issues in that person's life; makes it increasingly difficult for that person to own those issues. It was hard for me. It would have been twice as hard for Raymond. It is extremely difficult for someone with a severely damaged self-esteem, to admit they have a problem worthy of seeing a counselor. But this kind of admission and humility is the only thing that will open the door for repair in a person's life.

4) THE DEVIL'S DEVICES

In First and Second Corinthians Paul addresses an incident that he culminates in 2 Corinthians 2:11 with these words, *"for we are not ignorant of his* (Satan's) *devices."*

The device he referred to is a heart to forgive and reconcile. In the end of the story we saw forgiveness take place in a powerful way from the church toward Raymond. But I am greatly convinced that a lack of forgiveness and reconciliation in Raymond's heart carried enormous responsibility for the escalation of the whole incident.

First, Raymond held resentment in his heart for his father. He talked about it often and with great frustration.

Over the years I have watched many issues arise in people's lives that would never be problems if those people had taken the time and made the hard choice to forgive their mothers or fathers or both, for treatment they received growing up. As much as abuse is wrong, damaging and cruel, victimized individuals must forgive or the resentment in their hearts will escalate and fester within them to the destruction of their own bodies, minds and souls.

Raymond never forgave. He just let resentment grow.

When victims forgive, many of the affects the child abuse could continue to have in their lives can be thwarted. That is one of the ways counseling can be of help to victims of abuse.

But even without counseling, a victimized individual can sidestep many of the consequences of his or her victimization by simply *letting it go*; by forgiving and releasing the abuser from the punishment of hatred. However, the one really being punished in hatred . . . is the *hater* . . . not the *hated*.

Raymond also never forgave whatever things were causing the ever-widening gap between him and Sarah. No doubt Sarah carried some responsibility in this as well. But instead of dealing a deathblow to their pride and humbly coming together in reconciliation, they allowed their pride to drive a wedge of separation between them. And they couldn't find enough humility in their hearts to keep the gap from growing greater and greater.

Paul's enlightening phrase about the devil's devices gives us great understanding. A regular and effective device of the enemy is non-reconciliation and unforgiveness. If we allow this device of the enemies to linger in our relationships with anyone, let alone key people in our lives, we are headed for great amounts of sorrow and we can expect to suffer some severe results.

Forgiveness is holy. It is a divine trait offered from divinely influenced people. It has its source in God Himself. God sent his Son to die upon a cross so that the forgiveness of God for man's sins could happen. God paid the ultimate price to forgive us. He asks for us to follow His example by forgiving one another (Matthew 18:23-35).

The amount of unforgiveness in our world is scary. Its totals would be hard to chart because many won't admit they have it. And many more have, in their denial, redefined it so that they aren't sure what unforgiveness actually is.

Many more live with great amounts of bitterness for a few, or several people in their lives—and they do so with a settled conviction that their unforgiveness is justified. They justify it in their own minds because of the magnitude of the offence that was levied against them by the people they hate.

Still others have a sense in their hearts that what they feel toward their boss, their parents, their ex-business partner, their neighbor, their cousin or their *former* friend—isn't right; but they can't muster the humility to let it go. The result is bitterness, alienation, non-reconciliation, resentment and unforgiveness that hang over our world like a dark ominous cloud.

Even Christians, who are supposed to have the wherewithal to forgive others, find it easier to talk about than to do. That is why Jesus and the prominent writers in the New Testament address the subject with insistence and regularity.

That is also why what happened on Day Nine at the end of the church service was so miraculous. Let me acknowledge an obvious fact before I go on. Raymond's responsibility in the death of his daughter and in the depth of his sin and poor judgment did not have to do with loss and betrayal that was intimately connected to those who forgave him. In other words, Christina was Raymond's and Sarah's daughter—no one else's. Raymond's sin was his and no one else's and his betrayal wasn't really pointed in the direction of his forgivers. Therefore, some may feel their forgiveness of him wasn't that miraculous.

But in a church that is made up of godly people there is a sense of family, and loyalty, and trust, and faith that believers have in each other. People in churches really consider other adults to be their brothers and sisters in the Lord. That is, God is their father and Jesus, as the Son, is their brother; making all of us brothers and sisters of and in Christ. We are all sons and daughters of God. We are truly family. We don't live together in the same house and sleep in adjoining bedrooms. But in a very real sense, we are all related. And children of a family in a church tend to be children of the church family as well. A kind of ownership develops in the hearts of many for the children in the church.

That is the way our church felt in the service on Day Nine. Raymond, Sarah and Christina were part of the family.

Raymond, who was one of ours, and his sin, had carried direct responsibility for the brutal slaying of another one of ours—not just in our church, but also in the body of Christ. Make no mistake about it…people were angry. I had personally talked with some who were.

And yet, people felt the restraint on their hearts to forgive . . . as long as the proper posture was present in Raymond's heart. They knew forgiveness was a clear directive from God's word. The Spirit of God in every believer's heart was leading that way because God never leads in a way that moves in a direction contrary to His word. Raymond had pled for forgiveness and he was clearly a broken and humbled—even humiliated—man. All the potential for people to reject Raymond's request was present and all the elements to forgive were present. But it was a miracle of Christ's love in the collective hearts of the people that forgave Raymond.

The result was; Raymond and Sarah were able to have a church family to help them work through their pain. And they had access to an environment of love and acceptance in their church to assist them as they sought healing and tried to put their lives back together. In the chapter *Every Day Since* we learned that Raymond and Sarah weren't able to take full advantage of this environment of love to help their relationship heal. But it was available to them none-the-less.

I don't know of any other organization where that could happen. Most groups, institutions, and even some churches I know of, would have several individuals who would resist forgiveness from the beginning. They might lip-service a kind of graciousness to start with because everyone was doing it. But in time, Raymond, and maybe Sarah as well, would have felt the oppressive weight of their overall disapproval. That is why it was so beautiful to observe people making what appeared to be, individual decisions to forgive Raymond.

Who are you choosing to not forgive? The awe-inspiring holiness of God manifests itself when we forgive. Jesus said (my paraphrase) . . . *anyone can hate, only godly people can forgive* (Matthew 5:46). Powerful people are those who are humble enough to forgive. Weak people are those who are too prideful to forgive. Will you allow God's strength to live through you to forgive?

5) MANIPULATION AND CONTROL

are the practices of people who feel as though they have little control of their own emotional make-ups. We have all encountered, if only in the viewing of a movie, threats of injury or some other more severe consequence.

I can remember as a teenager being threatened by a bully for looking at him in the wrong way and at the time his threats were very persuasive. I had no interest in being pulverized by a greaser regardless of how weak his reason and character was for threatening me. However, most social experts will say that bullies were probably bullied themselves first. Consequently, to reclaim a sense of power, they bully others.

Inherent in my experience is the basis for the out of control controlling we saw in the story. People who have experienced the awful feeling of having their control aggressively and maliciously pried out of their hands—and who have been made to live under that oppressive power for any length of time—will often turn around and wield it themselves on anyone they can control. They do it in order to regain a sense of power that they perceive has been taken from them.

But the reality is, people who are weak in character, or personal confidence, or spirituality, or all the above; threaten physical displays of power or harm. It is a proclamation of their inability to control a situation with conventional, ethical and moral means.

Manipulation and power displays of control are not innate abilities found in people. They are learned. No doubt Daniel learned these abilities growing up and acquired additional lessons for their development in whatever lifestyle he led that landed him in prison before he met Raymond. And then I'm sure the state penitentiary helped to hone his skills in this area as well. It was all in preparation for the oppression he heaped on the Gils, and the dastardly deed he committed on Day Seven in the story.

There are two primary relational patterns of functioning in the world. One is governed by love and integrity. It is God's pattern for us. The other seems to invert all of love and integrity's tendencies into an opposite but parallel universe of functionality.

The second "Back to the Future" movie in the nineteen-eighties alluded to a fantasy version of this universe. In the movie they called it a parallel universe. It was science fictional and outside the realm of natural possibilities but contains an element of truth.

It suggested that a universe that is identical to, and parallel to ours, exists apart from our knowledge. Instead of being good, however, it is evil. Instead of it being a world governed by morality, good choices and good results; it is governed by bad, evil and immoral choices and results.

Well, in the real world, a similar system exists. It is a system in which people try to function by a completely different set of values than love and integrity. In this evil system people lie, use others, manipulate, cheat, control, threaten, play both ends against the middle, pull power plays, hide the truth and use all manner non-holy practices to accomplish the way of existence they call life.

A man named Andrew was referred to me through a prison outreach ministry. He was coming out of jail and onto parole and needed a church to help him. However, Andrew couldn't handle life on the streets because his intellect, emotions and will were programmed by a system of functioning that he had learned in his less than adequate upbringing, and his twenty-five year-long in and out of prison pattern.

Andrew lived in the other universe. He had given his life to Christ but didn't really know how to allow God's love and integrity to guide his choices. Instead, he relied on values inherent in the universe he had functioned in his whole life, to help him determine his choices. Consequently, from the time I was introduced to him; Andrew was in prison for two months and out for four . . . in for six months and out for one . . . in for nine months and out for three.

At the beginning of his last time out, I had a serious talk with Andrew about the source of the values and thought processes he was using to make his choices while he was on the outside. I talked to him about using integrity and honesty to get by instead of manipulating the system. I talked to him about living so that no one could point blame at him instead of walking a tightrope of lies and deceit. I talked with him about the value system he was using to help him choose the kind of people he would form relationships with. In short, I told him his whole universe of function ability was flawed and unless he made some serious mindset changes, he would be in and out of prison his whole life.

That is a picture of Daniel's control over Raymond. He was drawing from all he knew. He was using values and thought processes he learned from the evil and parallel universe he had been a part of his whole life. As far as Daniel was concerned, there was no other way to handle the situation but to take control, and do so with the skills he had picked up in the universe he lived in. And when his tactics didn't produce the desired results, he resorted to the wickedest device in his universe . . . murder.

Interestingly, Raymond had been dabbling in this alternate universe of functionality as well. He was thinking hide, shame, lie, cover up, don't snitch on a friend and trust a scoundrel. It was almost as though a tragedy was destined to occur. With both of these men engaging in choices and ideas that proceeded from the *dark side* of things . . . how could it be avoided?

Naturally the other universe of functionality is marked by God's approval and his presence. It is characterized by mercy, truth, integrity, honesty and love. It is one that is passionately desired by people like Daniel and Andrew but seems to be illusive and unachievable because it is so foreign to their ways of operating.

I am happy to say, Andrew did get the message. He grabbed hold of life in "The Light" and the last I heard is successfully making a value transition from dark to light. For Daniel, it was too late; at least to prevent a descent to the very dregs of his universe.

Any wickedness we experiment with such as threats, lying, hiding the truth, manipulation and so forth; will create sorrow, trouble and pain in our lives. But that's not all. When we find ourselves trying out these kinds of evils, we dabble in a universe capable of wickedness we can't even imagine.

6) Choosing Healthy Relationships

The Bible says, *"Bad company corrupts good character"* (I Corinthians 15:33 NIV). In the story I think anyone could see Raymond made a bad relationship choice, and most of us saw the foolhardiness of hooking up with a sordid character like Daniel Rogers. But folks connect with questionable people every day and as a result lose entire portions of their lives to the bad choices people like that lead them into.

When I was a senior in high school, a new kid moved into town. I can't remember how we got together, but once we did the rest of my senior year was lost. To be honest, I was leaning in a direction that wasn't the best anyway, but I didn't need the encouragement. In relationship with this person my grades went south fast. At the end of the year I barely had enough credits to graduate. With this person coaxing me, I started drinking heavily. I broke up with my girlfriend (now my wife – we got back together). I engaged in minor criminal activity and in short, I almost squandered my one and only life.

Since this experience I have been cautious as to the kind of people I choose as friends. A few times I have found myself connected with people that turned out to be stuck in non-growth . . . and not so good for me. But at a certain point, I felt no shame to leave them behind when I found myself growing beyond them in my life and spiritual maturity.

What are some of the warning signs of bad company?

Where you find them. There should have been flags, caution lights, sirens and warning signals going off for Raymond when he found Daniel at the porn house. But there wasn't. Or, he was so blinded he couldn't detect them. But if we find someone at a pornographic bookshop, a bar, a strip club, or some other dive, it should at least caution us to walk carefully into a close relationship with the person.

Their background. Prison should be a dead give away. Be careful if the person you are feeling inclined to connect with has been in jail for any length of time or has a record. There are exceptions but prison quite often means trouble. My relationship with Andrew was different. I was a spiritual mentor for him, and I never considered making him a close friend or confidant. The Bible's warning is, "Do not be unequally yoked together with unbelievers," (II Co. 6:14). But there are other warning signs such as sexual looseness, job after job, no job for a long time, vague information about their background, etc.

Their relationship with integrity. Does the person lie, compromise truth or tell tall tales? Do they cheat, steal, have angry outbursts, or meddle with the occult? I am not saying you should treat them like an untouchable. But you should never be quick to make them your close and trusted friend.

7) THE DESTRUCTIVE CONSEQUENCES OF A NEGATIVE AND CRITICAL SPIRIT.

Having been the pastor and point leader of a group of people for many years, I have sat in the hot seat of criticism often. It goes with the territory. People in churches, and for that matter all organizations, find fault. And people always seem to feel that their criticism must be the good kind because *they* could never be the kind of persons who engaged in the bad kind. The good kind of course is constructive criticism.

But I have found that the darkness that dwells within all people has a way of convincing us that our malicious tendencies are quite righteous. So, when we malign someone with unholy intentions and in unrighteous ways, we are blindly able to justify what we have just done as a perfectly acceptable action. People, families, churches and God's kingdom in general, pays a huge price for these self-deceptions.

This is not a discussion about constructive and right spirited criticism. So, I don't want to spend great amounts of time discussing it. But just to say, most leaders are discerning enough to detect from which spirit criticism comes. Sometimes a leader has his or her own self-esteem issues and is overly threatened by even good criticism; but the primary problem with criticism doesn't lie here. It lies in the darkness within all of us that desires to stand against and find fault with anything and everything.

Three primary issues cause negativity and a critical spirit.

Anger – is quite often fueling the critical spirit. People, who have been abused, victimized, abandoned, or rejected in some way, will be quick to find fault. Solomon advises, *"Make no friendship with an angry man, and with a furious man do not go. Lest you learn his ways and set a snare for your soul"* (Proverbs 22:24-25).

I once knew a young man who had been severely abused verbally and physically as a regular practice by his father. His father constantly belittled his son for failures, errant remarks, mistakes and other childish blunders. The result was an incredible amount of underlying anger in this young man. He was possibly the angriest man I have ever met. As a result, he had a habit of treating other people who blundered in any slight way, with a great deal of accusatory contempt. He would belittle people with disgust and distain for their *stupid* mistakes, their *stupid* ways, and their *stupid-ness*.

You can see his sub-conscious reasoning, can't you? If he can feel that other people are stupid, it helps him to feel better about the crushed spirit he carries around with him every day. This practice of belittling the intelligence of everyone who blunders is not unusual with those possessing angry spirits. People, who grew up in environments that were less than functional, are often angry and take out their anger on the mistakes of others, all to bring peace to their own troubled psyches.

Discontentedness – often, is also at the heart of negative criticism. In a passage about contentment, Paul advises believers to *"lead a quiet life, mind their own business, and to work with their hands"* (I Thessalonians 4:11). This is in sharp contrast to the *busy-body-ness* we see in many environments, and even Christian environments. Paul was challenging people to not put their noses into other people's business to criticize, find fault, poke fun at, put down or point blame at other people. What is at the root of much of the busy-body-ness in people's lives? It is simply . . . discontentedness in their hearts.

The scripture is saying godly people shouldn't be this way. We should be happy contented folks, just minding our own business because we find our contentment in our relationship with Christ (Colossians 2:10). We don't find our joy in a bit of juicy gossip or an act of criticizing another.

Poor Self-Image. This was the biggest problem in Raymond's life. His father had so beat him down with disapproval, Raymond found himself groping for every desperate straw he could find to help him feel good about himself. You know the routine, don't you? We all have the propensity within us to put someone else down—or tear someone else apart—just because it makes us feel better about ourselves. Then, when we are able to tell someone else and get a consensus from that person, it makes us feel even better. Thus, we have the basis for a great deal of the criticism that inundates our world.

But more sinister than the causes of criticism, are its consequences. I alluded to a few in the story.

One was *the alienation Raymond felt* from people who could act as accountability friends to him. With his critical activity, Raymond alienated himself from men mature enough to challenge him spiritually. This happens with great regularity. Critical people gravitate to critical people. Negative individuals tend to be self-absorbed and not at all into the growth of the people they spend their time with. They just sit around and tear down. They aren't at a place where they care about or notice the spiritual deficiencies of their friends. They only see the flaws of the objects of their criticisms.

Another result of criticism is *the loss of harmony in the church*. This is huge since no church sees any significant spiritual growth that is encumbered by the distraction of critical spirits. Our church recognized this with Raymond and was one critical incident away from asking him to leave so that our church wouldn't be affected by that distraction any more.

But churches all over our world are so hindered. People are negative and critical. Pastors are at a loss as to what to do about it. And churches are stagnant and declining because the crippling and oppressive spirit of criticism drives people away.

In my book *Beautiful Behaviors*, I deal more exhaustively with biblical methods and solutions about how to eliminate this dilemma from the church environment, though I don't have time to address that here. Yet, disharmony in the church is clearly an ugly result of a critical spirit. It is frightening to me to think about how some people are going to stand before the Lord some day, having allowed the ugliness within them to divide Christ's church.

The other consequence of criticism, one I also alluded to in the story; is, in my estimation, the most unsettling of all:

the quenching of spiritual receptivity in an otherwise tender and teachable life.

I am reminded of Jesus' warning to those who harm little children. *"And whoever causes one of these little ones who believe in me to stumble, it would be better for him if a millstone were hung around his neck, and he were thrown into the sea"* (Mark 9:42). This scripture should at least cause us to sit up and take notice when we are tempted to criticize in front of others; whether it is in front of people in the church, our spouses or our children. We should ask ourselves . . . *is the criticism I am about to levy going to cause these people to sin or stumble in their hearts before the Lord? And if it is, how will I ever give righteous account of myself before God?*

Never in all my years in the ministry, have I ever felt the eerie feeling I did when I considered Raymond's criticism . . . Christina's support of her father's attitude in the youth question and answer time . . . the barriers I felt in Christina's heart toward me as a result...Christina's unwillingness to heed my warnings . . . and then her death. I don't think I will ever get over the implications of that.

To be honest, I can't say for certain that Christina's death was the direct result of her loss of respect for me resulting from her father's critical attitude in the church. But the appearance is certainly there. And the possibility it had some influence . . . in my opinion, is high.

But that aside, I have encountered similar situations over the years where parents and spouses have stained their family members respect for the messenger with their critical spirits; to the degree that the influenced family members couldn't receive any ministry from that messenger. They would sit in church and as ministry was presented, family members would just resist.

In a world where respect for the message and the messenger is greatly waning, I'm not sure people, even our own family members, can afford for us to taint their ability to receive the gospel any more. Receptive hearts in our children or our spouses may be the last hope for some of them to come to the Lord or draw closer to Him. If our critical spirit spoils their receptivity, what hope is left?

Destructive criticism in the home provides family members with two negative encouragements.

First, it gives *permission* for family members to do the same and feel the same. Every heart possesses the carnal inclination to criticize and find fault. So depraved are we, that we are capable of finding error and passing judgment on things that deserve no condemnation. We are all capable of serious negativity...our kids and spouses too. All they need to become some of the most destructive gossips and faultfinders in the church, or for that matter any other organization they are a part of, is permission. Parents and spouses give permission when they do it themselves.

When Raymond ravaged the church with his tongue, heart and soul, and did so in the presence of Christina, he gave her permission to do the same; but along with her freedom to follow in her father's critical footsteps, came a closed heart to the things of God—and its messenger. Did Raymond foresee it? Probably not! But it happened just the same.

Second, criticism before family members provides for them a *model* to follow. The strongest teacher in the home is example. If you want your child to serve God . . . then you serve God. If you want your child to obey the law . . . then you obey the law. If you want your child to be a responsible citizen...then you be a responsible citizen. If you want your child to be a disparaging person; criticizing, condemning and finding fault with everything and everyone in his or her life, all you must do is be that yourself. And with your example . . . they may even outdo you.

It is my hope that you would resist and avoid this critical tendency that is in all of us, as you would the Black Plague; because it is all ready an epidemic in our world. The news media has made it the most dominant thing they do.

Resist it in your home. Resist it in your church. Resist it in all your relationships and dealings with people. It is one of Satan's most widespread and effective devices. In so doing, perhaps you can eliminate it out of your family, church and relational circles. It may not change the world, but it will change yours. And that is a start.

8) HUMILITY

I have never seen a person humbled as completely as Raymond was by the end of this story. We can understand why. His actions had direct bearing on his daughter's brutal death.

I have always felt that if we don't permit ourselves to become humble, God will permit us to *be* humbled. In other words, He will allow humbling circumstances to come our way. You see, God looks at humility in completely different ways than we humans. Most people are deathly afraid of owning embarrassing responsibility or allowing anything to happen that will bring on the state of humility. Everyone wants to save face . . . put on a strong front . . . keep a stiff upper lip, because the values of our world find as their leader . . . pride. And pride resists being the underdog, the weakling, the one walked on or being humiliated.

But humility is a healthy, wholesome, revitalizing and renewing place of being. The Bible says when we are humble before God, we can become stronger than if we try to be strong in ourselves (2 Corinthians 12:9). And because we are humble before the Lord, there is a peace that we feel, and we feel a kind of strength.

Paul the apostle actually welcomed humbling circumstances because he knew that the more of himself, he could get out of the way the closer he could be to the Lord, and stronger he could be in the Lord. So, he chose to gladly accept humble circumstances because they would make him a stronger and better person than if he tried to be strong in his own might.

Humility doesn't mean weak and walked on. It means we aren't impressed with ourselves, but we are impressed with God and what He is able to do in our lives if we let Him; and *letting Him* means being humble before Him.

In confirmation James says, *"Humble yourself in the sight of the Lord, and he will lift you up"* (James 4:10). And that's the way it should be. Humbling yourself and God lifting you up . . . is better than you lifting yourself up and God needing to humble you. But He will if He needs to.

How much better it is when we humble ourselves and allow God to lift us up. But if we aren't able to humble ourselves, God may choose to humble us. Wise is the person who endeavors to be humble, before God would choose for that person to be humbled.

Can you imagine yourself in the place of a humiliation as intense as Raymond experienced? Would God do that with you? I don't know, but He allowed it with Raymond. What might God have to allow for you to be humbled enough to trust His ways for your life?

9) BORN AGAIN.

It was Jesus who said, *"You must be born again, or you cannot see the kingdom of God"* (John 3:3). He was simply describing the process of regeneration and new life that must occur for one to become a true child of God. You see, becoming a Christian isn't a family tradition, a mental ascent or a decision to attend a church rather than a synagogue or masque. Becoming a Christian involves a decision to embrace Christ followed by a transformation experience only God's Spirit can give. Jesus called it *born again* or *born of the spirit* (John. 3:6). Paul called it *a spiritual death and resurrection* (Romans 6:4), and in another place, *a new creation* (2 Corinthians 5:17), and in still another place *putting on the new man* (Ephesians 4:24).

No matter what you call it, only God can give it. It seems that when a person comes to a place of full surrender and ownership of his or her sinfulness before God—and when that person completely and genuinely repents of being a sinner—the Spirit of God Himself enters the person's heart. When that happens, a divine surge of spiritual life enters that person for the purpose of transformation. This occurs, and is felt, as soon as that person opens his or her heart to the Lord. And instantly the transformation begins. There's a heart change. There's a mind change. There's a value change. There's a love change. There's a joy change. There's a will change. With these changes, in time, other more visible transformations begin to take place.

A young woman named Heidi was invited to our church service one Easter. She was very hungry for some direction and fulfillment in her life. She had been raised in a church that had taught the biblical idea of born again through relationship with Jesus Christ, but she had never experienced it for herself. Since her early church and Christian experiences had not presented her with any lasting meaning, she wandered away from the church. Her wandering caused her to become mixed up in lifestyles and relationships that were unfulfilling and purposeless. That is why she was open to coming to church when someone invited her.

At the end of the service that day I told the people how to begin a relationship with Jesus Christ if they wanted to do that and dismissed the service.

The next day Heidi was engaged in her usual routine, running ten miles around a nearby reservoir. She was a tri-athlete and a gifted one at that. As she ran, while pondering her aimless life, she recalled my description of how to become a Christian. And this is what she said to herself as she ran.

"Chris said if I am honestly sorry for my sins and I surrender my life to Jesus and invite Him into my life to be my Lord and Savior, He'll come, and I will become a Christian. If that's all there is to it, then what do I have to lose? If nothing happens, I'll be just as I am right now. If it works, it might be just what I need."

So, she did. As Heidi ran, she said with as much sincerity as she could muster in a heavenward direction, "Jesus I am truly sorry for my sins. Please forgive me. I surrender my life to You, and I invite You into my life to be my Lord and Savior."

As soon as she said this, she began to feel a weight come off her shoulders as she ran. A song popped into her head that she remembered from her Sunday school days growing up. She began to sing it though she couldn't recall all the words. But she repeated what she remembered over and over again.

"Every morning is Easter morning from now on. Every day is resurrection day the past is over and gone."

As she sang, she ran faster. And as she ran faster, she felt lighter. She felt as though she was running about three feet above the ground. The faster she ran the louder she sang, and tears of joy began pouring from her eyes as she did so.

At a certain point she realized she was passing other runners who were running both ways, while she was singing and crying with all her might. The thought came into her mind, "they must think I am nuts," but decided she didn't care. At that moment she felt so clean . . . so forgiven . . . so accepted by God . . . so brand new . . . she didn't want to stop.

Heidi was born again by the Spirit of God. This wasn't some new-fangled idea that the gospel writer thought up as he wrote. Five hundred years before Christ, Ezekiel prophesied from God's own mouth that this would be the kind of experience that would characterize the true people of God. He said, *"I will give you a new heart and put a new spirit within you. I will take the heart of stone out of your flesh. I will put my Spirit within you and cause you to walk in my statutes, and you will keep my judgments and do them"* (Ezekiel 36:26-27).

Once a person such as Heidi has become personally broken and repentant to the place where God enters that life by His Spirit; that Spirit gives one a new power to say no to sin (Romans 6:2).

When Raymond invited Christ into his life, it seems he did it like many do. He wanted to do it, but he wasn't broken enough, or surrendered enough, to come to the place where full regeneration could occur. He told me that he never experienced anything like the born-again experience.

Without this power to discern and say no to sin, it isn't unusual that he would be able to condone, justify and rationalize all manner of sinful and questionable activity in his life; lies, unfaithfulness, lust, pornography criticism and so-forth. With the Spirit in his life, he would have had a fighting chance against the perils of sin. And he would have had a more discerning heart to detect what was sin.

And so will you. If you think yourself a Christian, or desire to be one; settle for nothing less than God's divine regeneration package—the born again—born of the Spirit experience. Accept nothing less because nothing less will make you a bona-fide Christian. And nothing less will give you the power to overcome the nagging temptations that Satan and our flesh throws at us every single day.

The Bible tells us that we will never overcome sin completely in this life because we have bodies of flesh and sin will always linger in our hearts. But with God's Spirit in us to help us, we can have the upper hand.

10) TRUTH HIDING

At a certain point in the ordeal, even Raymond recognized the folly of him continuing to hide his affair with Daniel from Sarah—or for that matter from anyone else. But Raymond was deceived on several levels. He thought he could keep his wife and family and have Daniel too. He thought he could hide it all from his family and church. He thought if he told Daniel to keep the relationship quiet, he would. He thought Daniel's love for him was true love. He thought Daniel's threats were empty. It was all a deception to Raymond.

Huge amounts of shame were piled up in Raymond's heart. That is why he was so deceived that *hiding things* would actually work, and that the best thing to do was to hide.

It is a commentary on the origin of sin in our world and in our hearts. Adam and Eve were ashamed of both their sin and its outcome, so they hid in the bushes. And hiding did no good. God saw, each other saw, and they, themselves saw. It remains the same for all of us. And yet, we humans continue to hide our sin and shame.

The Bible uses the image of darkness and the night to describe the deceptiveness of sin and its propensity to try and hide itself.

"The way of the wicked is like darkness; they do not know what makes them stumble" (Proverbs 4:19). *"And this is the condemnation, that the light has come into the world, and men loved darkness rather than light, because their deeds were evil. For everyone practicing evil hates the light and does not come to the light, lest his deeds should be exposed. But he who does the truth comes to the light, that his deeds may be clearly seen, that they have been done in God"* (John 3:19-21).

On the other hand, the Bible depicts God as the light that, not only exposes the darkness and man's evil deeds; He brings about the freedom of truth.

Here is what sin and shame does. It confuses so that there is great complexity concerning wise and proper choices. And thus, we have the quip...*oh what a tangled web we weave when we practice to deceive.*

Raymond started hiding, but he didn't foresee or discern Daniel's inclination to control and manipulate. Nor did he anticipate the degree to which Daniel could go in his power plays. It was all part of the deception.

Then Daniel's control started to kick into high gear. First, "If you don't spend time with me, I'll tell." Then, "If you don't leave your wife, I'll tell her and your church about us." Next, "If you don't stay with me, I'll smear your reputation to your customers and to your whole city." And finally, "If you break my heart, you and your family will pay a huge price."

Long before the threats moved from mild to hot, Raymond's shame mingled with his fear, combined with his frantic hopes to keep it all hidden, had him in such a state of confusion, his decisions were purely reactionary. Psalms 35:6 says, *"His way was dark and slippery."* So confused and uncertain was Raymond on this dark and treacherous path, it was almost certain that he would slip and fall to a disastrous outcome.

Truth and sin-hiding often seems like the best solution at the moment of our indiscretions. But it immediately plunges our lives into perilous possibilities. Instead of clear vision—darkness, blindness, deception and confusion instantly become the ruling factors in the situation. What hope could there be for a positive outcome?

11) LIFESTYLES

In Day One, I suggested that a primary factor causing Raymond to consider becoming gay was related to a bruise on his soul from his childhood years. I wasn't trying to say that the sources of all gay tendencies in people are similar experiences. It just seemed that this could well have been the source of Raymond's gravitation in this direction. There are many other possible sources influencing people to try and adopt the gay option as a lifestyle, though I won't take the time to address them here.

In every church where I have been pastor, there have been people who had been involved in the gay or lesbian lifestyle. Each shared with us their inclination in that direction so that we were aware. They felt comfortable enough to come to our church because they sensed acceptance from us as their pastors, and from the overall environment emitted by our people.

To clarify, they weren't gays or lesbians who were currently pursuing that lifestyle. They were people who felt God's guidance to come out of the lifestyle to move in a different direction. But they came to our church because it was one of the few churches where they could find acceptance.

For a reason I do not understand, some Christians struggle to accept anyone who has been connected to the LGBT lifestyles. But that is not the heart of God.

God's door is wide open to all people regardless of their lifestyle.

Actually, God invites all people to come to Him just as they are. He doesn't ask people to clean up their acts before they come because He knows, without His Spirit living in their lives, there is no power to clean up anything. So, He invites everyone to come to Him just the way they are. And when they come, broken and humble, in keeping with His promise, He places His Spirit inside of them (Ephesians 1:13).

So, God loves and accepts everyone as they are. This is the way He deals with all manner of people...alcoholics, drug addicts and dealers, adulterers, liars, cheaters and non-integrals of every kind. He even accepts murderers, and rapists, and extortionists, and child abusers in the same way. He invites all people to come to Him as they are. He doesn't reject them because of their past failures and sinful behaviors. He accepts them despite what they have done.

Then, when His Spirit enters their hearts at conversion, God begins to lead them into His will for their lives by the same Spirit (John. 16:13). But God is love; and His mercy, grace, forgiveness and understanding surrounds all His dealings with people.

God's Spirit lovingly nudges transformation in our inward perceptions, values, thought processes and mindsets first. Then He lovingly nudges change outwardly. With most this takes time, and as time passes and change occurs gradually, God is patient and accepting.

Many people, who claim to be Christians, have insensitively and inaccurately painted an angry judgmental picture of God toward gays. As well, they communicate a kind of disgust that they themselves have for gays and lesbians in the process. But these Christians are not in touch with the compassionate and redemptive side of God's heart.

They are more like an extremist break-off from Christianity. They are thinking human judgment and self-righteousness. They aren't thinking divine love and grace. As a result, many in the LGBT community hate all Christians and all churches because they think these people represent the feelings of every other Christian.

In the story you saw an example of a group of Christians who reflected the heart of God who loved a man who wasn't just involved with a gay man. He had carelessly allowed his inclination to lure a blatant criminal (who happened to be gay) into murdering one of their own. And yet they accepted him, forgave him and received him back into their fold. That is the heart of God.

If you are a Christian who struggles to accept and love people in the LGBT community, please, fall on your knees and ask God to give you the portion of His heart that loves and receives them. If you are gay or lesbian, be convinced of only one thing. God loves and wants you to come to Him.

12) GOD'S SOVEREIGNTY

This is our last lesson, which we will use to conclude. The subject of God's sovereignty is a great source of confusion in the minds of people who have serious doubts about God. Even for some of us more seasoned believers, we don't like to discuss God's sovereignty because the whole concept doesn't fit into our comfortable theological patterns of thinking.

We don't know how to treat the idea: *God can do what He wants, how, when and where He wants to do it.* It throws off our methodologies of how we understand the actions of a deity who also claims to be holy. Could God, such as is described in the Bible, really allow a murder as horrific as the one that took Christina's life, and in its process, use it to save a teenage girl eternally? Could God's love be so illogical as to appear to manipulate hate . . . in order to accomplish His love?

Every generation finds itself questioning a God who appears to allow war and use it to manipulate His will. Human doubts along these lines have their origins in the Old Testament, with God instructing His people to "wipe out" their enemies for His Glory. And those doubts have not ceased to this day. We must remember, however, that there are many traits about an infinite God that our finite minds will never have comprehension of in this life. The Bible says, *"One day we will know"* (I Corinthians 13:12). But many truths about Him, we will never know, or understand, in this era we call human history.

As all of this relates to Christina, only God knew what circumstances would be persuasive enough for her heart to be softened toward God in a way that would draw her to Him. Only God knew that her death by sudden and unforeseen murder could be what would be necessary to bring her safely into His eternal kingdom.

We aren't certain Christina is in heaven, but Sarah is convinced she is. She is the one who saw her heart soften over the week. I am satisfied to trust Sarah's assessment. Could God's intricate knowledge of Christina's mind and future cause Him to graciously take her to be with him before she would fall, so, He allowed the murder?

I do know Sarah was desperately praying for her soul. Certainly, God knows that the importance of eternal life far supersedes the importance of temporal life, even if we don't. Besides, only a holy God can see the future with enough understanding of its causes and outcomes to predict it, and then orchestrate it, even if the prediction may raise questions about His holiness. God's words to Job come to mind. *"Why are you using your ignorance to deny my providence?"* (Job 38:2 LB)

Many would argue . . . *No, something such as this isn't possible with a holy God. A perfectly pure God could never allow such a twist of theological fate.* But stranger things have seemed to occur even in the Bible; and God had no problem attributing their outcome to the work of His hand. The Book of Esther is one shining example. The heart of Pharaoh in Exodus being manipulated by God's hand is another.

It's so much easier to say . . . *Stuff like Christina's murder happens, and God can use it for His Glory.* Or . . . *God had nothing to do with the event whatsoever.* These answers are safe. They keep us within the parameters of orthodox reasoning.

However, I can't help but recall Job's words, *"Though God slay me, yet will I trust in Him"* (Job 13:15). Could the God who is the *"God of the living and not the dead"* (Matthew 22:32) slay someone for His purposes, or at least allow it? My faith begs, no screams, to be able to, with Job, trust God's sovereignty enough to allow Him the latitude to possess love and grace at a large enough level to be able to orchestrate a teenage girl's death because the only way she could be saved eternally was if it happened the way it did.

Maybe it did happen along the lines of one of the safe explanations we gave a moment ago. I'm OK with that too. But I prefer a God who is a little more beyond my ability to explain Him, and who is still holy. I prefer a God who has *"higher thoughts and higher ways"* (Isaiah 55:9) than ours. If we could comfortably explain and understand his ways, He wouldn't be as great as He is. He would be more human than divine.

This incident describes a God that is bigger than our ability to understand Him. He is the kind of God I want to serve. He is the kind of God I can believe in.

The End

But wait there's more...

EPILOG

I have read and re-read the story of *Murder in the Church* over and over for refining and editing purposes and I have never been able to read it without weeping at several different places. The sadness in the story, along with the remembrances of the events that come to me at different times, are often difficult to contain. I find myself overwhelmed with emotion. The story feels as painful to me when I read it as when I lived it.

When I interpret the events of this story and God's insertion into it, as well as the emotion it evokes in me; and then when I place it alongside the fact that I find myself coming back to it over and over for different reasons; I have to consider that it is a story that was intended to bring definition to my whole ministry.

The lessons in the story are so clear and timeless they move me even two decades after they happened. Furthermore, as I have ministered since then to people throughout my travels, the lessons keep coming up in the people's lives I serve; though happily, no other mishaps as shocking have taken place.

I wonder now and then if God had told me when He called me into His service that something like this was going to happen in some church I would lead, if I would have said yes to the call. Though it is impossible to speculate about this,

I would have to assume that I would have said yes. I assume this because it seems that I was supposed to experience it and . . . write about it. I know that sounds odd to people trying to understand how and why God does what He does. But I have quit trying to figure God out. As the word imports, *"His ways are higher than ours and are beyond our ability to figure out"* (Isaiah 55:9 – my paraphrase).

The family that experienced these tragic events was never the same. They have moved on, but the pain still remains and my heart hurts for them continually. Per their request, I have sheltered them from connection to the story by changing names, dates and locations. However, this story is no longer about them. It is about God and His purposes; and it is about the kinds of consequences that can happen to anyone unwilling to submit all their ways to Him.

SMALL GROUP DISCUSSION QUESTIONS ABOUT MURDER IN THE CHURCH

INTRODUCTION

The lessons in the final chapter of *Murder in the Church* offer opportunities for discussion and growth. But let me warn you, these questions will challenge you. They proceed straight from the author's experience and the sobering lessons he gleaned from the story.

These questions and studies are not designed for casual discussion. Some questions are very pointed. They aren't intended to embarrass anyone, but are designed for healing, deliverance and life-transformation. MITC (*Murder in the Church*) will change lives. These group studies are intended to facilitate that objective. Leaders; lead your group that way.

These questions are designed to follow after the reading of the book—lessons included. After each person in your group finishes the book, including the lessons in their entirety; that is when we would recommend that you begin your discussions and teachings about it. Begin with discussion about the overall story (the first discussion) and impressions people had as they read. Probing questions are provided for the first meeting of your group.

Some questions list several interrogations and discussion topics related to the main question. It is advised that leaders take their groups systematically through each discussion point because they are designed to cover the entire topic of the question.

The thirteen lessons provide the same number of weeks for reflection and discussion, causing the small group studies about this book to last a total of one quarter of a year.

We would suggest that each person in your group reread the week's lesson in preparation for that week's discussion. To save time and space, and to avoid redundancy, in this section *Murder in the Church* will be represented by MITC.

As much as we continually refer to this story as a book, we don't consider it to be a book as much as we consider it to be an experience. Our prayer is that you will grow from and be changed by the experience of MITC.

Small Group Discussion Questions About Murder in the Church

MITC

First Discussion – The Story

1. Do you consider it naïve to think: It is not possible for something like what happened in MITC could happen in your life or family? Discuss why you think it is or isn't naïve.

2. Discuss some of the elements of the story that exist in your life or the life of someone close to you; issues like, pornography, unhealthy relationships, criticism, control, marital coldness, un-forgiveness, poor parenting, etc.

3. When did you perceive that the perpetrator would take his revenge out on Raymond's daughter? Why

do you think you perceived it when you did? Or did you not see it coming at all? If this is so, why?

4. What situations do you see in your family or life that resemble scenarios from the story?

5. Has there ever been a person in your life that you feel was a bad relationship choice? Why were they a bad relationship choice? Is there anyone in your life now that isn't good for you?

6. What safeguards should you set in place to ensure something like this doesn't happen in your life or family?

7. Discuss the God-experiences in this story; the prophesy of Christina's death, the realization by the Author and his wife that the day of Christina's murder was the day God had prophesied, the presence of God in the service, and God's call for the author to write the book. Which seems the most miraculous to you and why?

8. Discuss the strategies performed in the story by the author and Sarah. Did they make mistakes? If so, what should they have done differently? What part did God play in the decisions that were made in MITC?

MITC

Second Discussion – 1st Lesson: Marriage
It is recommended that each group member reread this lesson in the book before they come to the study.

1. Do you have signs of coldness in your marriage relationship? What are they? What can you do to bring warmth to them?

2. Is nourishing and cherishing happening in your relationship? What will you do to change that?

3. What are the barriers to healing and intimate conversation happening in your marriage? How can you tear down some of these barriers?

4. What location can you feasibly identify and designate as your "porch swing", where healing and intimate conversation take place in your marriage? How will you make these conversations happen? How can you as a group partner together to see that happen for each other?

5. Do you see signs of the "empty nest syndrome" happening in your marriage relationship? If so, what are they? What will you do to turn the tide of this syndrome in your marriage?

6. Do you engage in pornography, or see signs of pornography usage in your spouse? If you do, what should you do? What can the people in your group do to work together to combat this problem in one another's marriage and family?

7. Do you have date nights in your marriage? If not, why?

MITC

Third Discussion – 2nd Lesson: Parenting
It is recommended that each group member reread this lesson in the book before they come to the study.

1. Do you use any language with your children that may be destructive to their self-esteem? Does anyone else in your household use abusive language in the environment of your family? What will you do about that?

2. What curse words have you used to communicate with or reprimand people in your household? Discuss with the group how any of these words may be damaging to them.

3. Have you ever been reprimanded with destructive words from your parents, boss or another authority figure in your life? Give examples. How did those words make you feel?

4. Do you know of any verbal, sexual, physical or emotional abuse that is happening with people you know? What should you do about it?

5. Are you aware of any ways in which you may be abusing your children, verbally, physically, sexually or emotionally? Discuss with the group what correct definitions of these abuses should be? Talk about what might be differences in our society's definition of emotional and verbal abuse and the Bible's definition. Use Ephesians 6:4 as a foundation for your discussion.

6. Do you have a working awareness of something like the "Affirmation Rule" in your parenting interactions with your children? Discuss current parenting laws that govern parenting procedures. Are you afraid to discipline your children for fear of your methods being perceived as abuse?

MITC

Fourth Discussion – 3rd Lesson: Emotionally Damaged*
It is recommended that each group member reread this lesson in the book before they come to the study.

1. Are you able to identify behaviors that may be connected to abuse you received growing up? If so,

what are they? How might these behaviors affect the people in your family? Discuss with the group what baggage you carry and how you may drop it on people in your family.

2. In Matthew 12:34 Jesus said, *"Out of the abundance of the heart the mouth speaks."* Discuss the latest words that came from your mouth that reflected an ugly heart issue within you.

3. Have you ever considered that some of your language and possible verbal abuse may require spiritual healing?

4. How is your self-esteem? On a continuum, with 1 being very low and 10 being high, give your self-esteem rating a number. Discuss with the group why you placed yourself where you did. Can you connect some of your behaviors with the rating you gave yourself?

5. Do you fear a person admitting that he or she has been emotionally damaged will cause people to label that person unstable? Discuss this fear. Is this fear a sign that someone has experienced some emotional trauma?

6. Do you have an idea how one who has been emotionally damaged by their childhood would go about obtaining healing? Share your answer with the group. Discuss how one would obtain a healing such as this?

7. Discuss the fears people feel about looking within to discover emotional wounds that may exist in their lives. Why are people afraid to look within?

* Consider using Chris Schimel's book *Once Broken* as a tool for emotional healing.

MITC

Fifth Discussion – 4th Lesson – The Devil's Devices
Forgiveness

It is recommended that each group member reread this lesson in the book before they come to the study.

1. Do you have anyone you need to forgive in your life? Anyone in your family of origin? Extended family? Immediate family? Your church? At work? Your neighborhood? Anyone else? If not, have you justified your interaction with them as something different than un-forgiveness? If so, discuss how your justification could in fact be un-forgiveness.

2. If the answer to any of the questions above is yes, how will you go about extending forgiveness? Which method will you use to contact them and begin the conversation; email, letter, text, Facebook, phone or in person?

3. Does anyone listed in the categories in question one have un-forgiveness for you? If so who? Since Jesus communicated in Matthew 18 that un-forgiveness of any kind between us and another is our responsibility to go to that person; how will you initiate the first contact: email, letter, text, Facebook, phone or in person?

4. Have you considered that your un-forgiveness creates spiritual bondage that hinders your life, family, relationships, church, etc. (Matthew 18:18)? Read this verse and discuss how this might be so.

5. After reading it, talk about how the parable Jesus tells in Matthew 18:23-35 relates to God's forgiveness of us through Jesus death on the cross. Talk about how it may relate to us forgiving those who

wrong us. Talk about how it may relate to spiritual bondage in our own lives.

6. Based on all the discussions above, talk about what importance Jesus places on forgiveness. Discuss how un-forgiveness provides a model and gives permission for people we lead or are close to us, to do the same.

MITC

Sixth Discussion – 5th Lesson – Control
It is recommended that each group member reread this lesson in the book before they come to the study.

1. Have you ever been mistreated by a bully? If so, tell about how it made you feel. If not, talk about someone you know who was bullied and how it made them feel.

2. Have you ever been a bully? If so, tell about why you think you were inclined to be this way. Discuss how it may have made the person you bullied feel.

3. Talk about how previously bullied people may find themselves relating to others. Discuss feeling powerful through overpowering others.

4. Talk about the two different universes of evil and good that people live in and how they play themselves out in our daily lives. Do you sometimes draw from behaviors inherent in the evil universe to accomplish things in your good universe? If so, give examples. How far have you gone into the evil universe to draw from its methodologies?

5. Have you ever manipulated your spouse to do things? In what ways? Do you feel it is a healthy way to accomplish your goals? Discuss other ways than manipulation, of coaxing people to do the things you want them to do.

6. Discuss how manipulation is a form of hatred rather than love.

7. Discuss how manipulation is a generational sin that will be visited on our children to the third and fourth generation (Deuteronomy 5:9). Talk about how manipulation will set an example for your children that they will follow even if they are trying their hardest to not do it. Talk about why manipulation and control may be a sin.

8. Talk about how even the smallest acts of manipulation produces resentment in others. How can you reverse this resentment?

MITC

Seventh Discussion – 6ᵗʰ Lesson Healthy Relationships
It is recommended that each group member reread this lesson in the book before they come to the study.

1. Have you ever made a bad relationship choice? Describe what made it a bad choice. Why do you think you chose to be with that person? Was there anything in your heart that was not right that went into making that friend-choice?

2. Have you ever reaped any bad results or consequences from a bad relationship choice? What were some of those consequences? What would you do differently if you had it to do over again?

3. What kind of criteria do you use when you are choosing people to form a relationship? Are your stipulations biblical? Are there stipulations that aren't biblical that are still good to consider? If so, what are they? What kinds of people should you not have as a friend?

4. How does concern for a person's soul play into choosing them as a close friend? At what point do you determine it is wiser to let a friendship go, though it may have bearing on that person's salvation.

5. Do you use the internet to search for friends? Before using the internet to find romance, what kinds of cautions should a person have in place? Should we all be open to new friends? Why or why not?

6. Should a Christian consider making a lost person a close friend? Should a Christian make an unbeliever a business partner? Why or why not?

7. Where is the best place to find a friend? Where is the worst place to find a friend? How much time should you take before you decide to make someone a close friend?

MITC

Eighth Discussion – 7ᵗʰ Lesson – Critical
It is recommended that each group member reread this lesson in the book before they come to the study.

1. Do you have a critical spirit? How you would define a critical spirit? What kind of criticism would you consider necessary?

2. What is the difference between a critical spirit and constructive criticism? Do you sometimes border on being more critical that you should and justify it by saying you were criticizing constructively?

3. Have you ever considered that your criticisms were sinful? What would you consider to be sinful criticism? List them.

4. Have you ever caught yourself while criticizing and determined that your criticisms were birthed out of a desire to put someone else down in order to make you feel better about yourself? Have you ever identified while criticizing, that the reason you were critical was because of your low self-esteem?

5. Have you ever considered that your tendency to be critical may set an example for your children to be that way as well? How do you feel about that? How do you feel about parents who engage in criticism when their children are present? Is this wrong or just normal for most families?

6. Have you ever thought about the possibility that your children can learn how to criticize from you, the same as they can learn how to handle their finances, drive a car or have manners?

7. Does a person with a critical spirit have anger issues? If so, in what ways?

8. Which is better, criticizing others outside of your children's hearing, or not criticizing at all? Do you think people who are more critical than others have this tendency because of heredity or because of sin? Could it be a generational sin?

MITC

Ninth Discussion – 8th Lesson – Humility

It is recommended that each group member reread this lesson in the book before they come to the study.

1. Have you ever been humbled to the place where you could not explain your actions away? If so, describe the incident to those in your group.

2. Discuss why it is so important to God that we are humble people.

3. Why is humility a healthy place for people to be? Discuss the relationship between humility and transparency.

4. Place your humility rating on a continuum from one to ten, ten being fully humble and one being fully prideful. Tell why you placed yourself where you did. Discuss what you need to do to raise your humility quotient. How will you keep pride at bay in your life?

5. Why is it so hard to discuss your own humility with people?

6. Discuss the difference between humble and self-degrading. Why is putting yourself down prideful rather than humble?

7. Discuss the difference between humble and weak. Discuss why humility is a sign of strength rather than weakness.

8. What would you do if you ever found yourself in a scenario as humbling as Raymond's? Explain why your answer is either humble or prideful.

MITC

Tenth Discussion – 9th Lesson – Born Again

It is recommended that each group member reread this lesson in the book before they come to the study.

1. Have you experienced being born again? Describe your born experience to others in the group. Tell why you believe yours was a genuine born-again experience. If you do not know if you have been born-again, be honest and share it with the others.

2. Do you feel the Holy Spirit dwells within you and is active in your daily walk with the Lord? If not, share that with the group. Talk with those in your group about how the Holy Spirit interacts with you in your daily life.

3. Discuss how your born-again experience was related to humility. Do you feel the same as you did when you were first born-again? What is different? What is the same?

4. Discuss whether Raymond was born-again. Cite reasons why he was or wasn't.

5. Is there a parallel in your experience in the Lord with Raymond's? If so, describe it to your group. If not, explain how yours is different.

6. How is your experience similar to Heidi's? How is it different? Discuss how the differences in your experience and hers qualify, or disqualify, your experience from being a genuine born-again experience.

7. Talk about how Raymond's lack of an active born-again experience may have contributed to the tragedy in the story. Talk about how and why your born-again experience could prevent possible tragedies in your life.

MITC

Eleventh Discussion – 10ᵗʰ Lesson – Truth Hiding
It is recommended that each group member reread this lesson in the book before they come to the study.

1. Are there any truths you are hiding from someone in your life? Are you brave enough to share them?

2. Have you ever had to lie to cover another lie? If you feel comfortable, share it.

3. Discuss the tangled web of lies in Raymond's situation as well as how and when he could have best curtailed the disaster with truth.

4. Discuss the different deceptions Raymond was believing mentioned in Lesson Nine. Which deceptions were the most severe and caused the greatest calamity in the story?

5. Discuss a time when you were deceived about something. How did that deception affect your life overall?

6. Talk about how Daniel was deceived and how it played into his controlling treatment of Raymond.

7. Talk about how Christina was deceived and what she may have been deceived about. Who was deceived more, Raymond, Daniel or Christina and why?

8. Discuss the role that shame played in the truth-hiding Raymond engaged in during the story. What is the relationship between truth-hiding and shame?

MITC

Twelfth Discussion – 11th Lesson – Lifestyles

It is recommended that each group member reread this lesson in the book before they come to the study.

1. Do you know someone who is gay or lesbian? Describe what your relationship with that person is like.

2. As a Christian, do you feel awkward with being or becoming a close friend with that person? If so, state why.

3. Discuss the author's statement in Lesson Ten, "God's door is wide open to gays." Do you agree? Why? Why not?

4. Do you agree with the author's statement, "God invites all people regardless of their backgrounds to come to Him as they are,"? Explain why you agree. Explain why you disagree.

5. Discuss this statement. "The reason some Christians have trouble with gays and lesbians has to do with the same reason the Pharisees had trouble with those they called sinners in Jesus day." How did Jesus feel about these Pharisees? How did Jesus feel about those the Pharisees called sinners?

6. When a person becomes a Christian God places His Holy Spirit in them (John 3). Do you trust the Holy Spirit's work in other people? Do you trust the Holy Spirit's work in your life? Why?

7. If someone from the LGBTQ+ community came to Christ, would you trust the Holy Spirit's work in them? Why? Why not?

8. What does the Bible say is the only un-pardonable transgression (Matthew 12:31-32)? Discuss how this answer can help you to be more receptive to those in the LGBTQ+ community?

MITC

Thirteen Discussion – 12th Lesson – God's Sovereignty
It is recommended that each group member reread this lesson in the book before they come to the study.

1. Do you agree with this statement: *"God can do what He wants, when He wants and where He wants?"* Why or why not?

2. Can God use a murder of a young girl to accomplish His will of bringing her to heaven? Discuss why you agree or do not agree.

3. Discuss the possibility that Christina's response to pray with her mom and dad and thank God for rescuing her Dad from Daniel could represent her getting her heart right before God. Is it possible? If so, how is it possible. Discuss Luke 23:42-43 regarding this.

4. Can God's love be so illogical as to appear to manipulate hate in order to accomplish his love?

5. Discuss Exodus 14:4 and Isaiah 55:9 in light of Christina's death and God's prediction to the author's wife that it would take place.

6. How does Job's statement in Job 13:15 relate Christina's death?

7. Discuss John 8:44 considering God's prediction and responsibility in Christina's murder. If people die in a battle God told Israel to engage in, who is the killer of the people; God, the soldiers, or Satan? Discuss your answers.

8. Discuss the statement: Eternal life is considerably more important than temporal life. Discuss why you agree or disagree.

9. Considering the implications of this Lesson and your discussions about it; do you feel you have a stronger grasp on God and His wisdom? Will you give God more latitude to be beyond our ability to comprehend? If so, tell why. If not share why.

OTHER BOOKS BY CHRIS SCHIMEL

I do, Do You?
Advice from God for Marital Success

This is a marriage-saver book. It is a companion book to Chris' book *Murder in the Church*. All the principles in *I Do, Do You?* are gleaned from God's Word. Most come from Ephesians 5:21-31, the premier passage in the Bible about marriage, but others are addressed. It is what is meant by the "God-advice" suggestion in the sub-title of the book. God wants marriages, which were His invention, to more than survive. He wants them to thrive. Who better to know how that can happen than the one who invented marriage and made its participants to function best in marriage His way? This book presents sound scriptural concepts that contain golden nuggets of truth that *if followed* will save and strengthen marriages. They will fan the early flames of love, rekindle otherwise cooling marriages, as well as rescue frigid unions on the verge of being frozen forever.

Once Broken
A Pathfinder to Emotional Healing and Health

Once Broken changed the author's life before it was ever a book. One day, after he had already become a Christian, had gone to Bible college and seminary, and had pastored churches for more than fifteen years, he woke up and realized: he was broken… and needed healing. The book takes readers seeking to find emotional healing with him down the same path he took to healing. It has already been the means many have used to find healing in Christ. It can also be considered a companion book to Chris' book *Murder in the Church* as it addresses a key cause for the tragedy of the story; emotional ill-health.

Touch One
How Much is One Soul Worth to God?

When an irate and possibly insane man showed up at Pastor Chris Schimel's church on what would have otherwise been a normal afternoon, the pastor felt his anxiety level rising and his time slipping away. When the man continued to visit over the months, and as the pastor became increasingly involved in the desperate man's life—it became crystal clear that God had placed that man in Pastor Chris' life for a reason. This book addresses the heart of ministry and is a delightful book for small group studies. With the purchase of five copies or more the study guide is free (first edition copies available for significant savings for a limited time).

Beautiful Behaviors
Christian Conduct So Normal It's Extreme

What makes the church beautiful? What causes Christians to appear beautiful to those outside the church? How can the church, the bride of Christ, develop beauty that reflects the glory and character of Christ, her Bridegroom? This book addresses how Christians and churches can be instruments of Christ's Beauty that attracts people to Him. This book is a favorite book of small group studies. With the purchase of five or more a study guide is free.

Between You and Me
Rescuing Relationships from Lifelessness

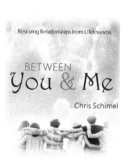

Between You and Me is an insightful "mini" E-book that could change all your relationships for the better. It contains six insightful chapters filled with hidden nuggets from God's Word that will make profound differences in your relationships. Because of its mini-size, it provides a concise package of six individual lessons; but if desired, could easily be lengthened into a twelve-lesson format by making each chapter stretch into two lessons of discussion. Discussion questions are included at the end of each chapter.

Lessons of the Fall
Building a Healthy Foundation for Living

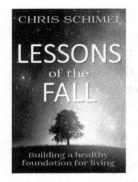

Lessons of the Fall is a profound book examining the inward emotional and practical implications of the fall of the human race into sin. If one thought the events of the first three chapters Genesis were just fairy tales, after working through this eye-opening and captivating book, those thoughts may disappear. Such subjects as blame, self-esteem, the rise of narcissism, sexual battles, the real curse, why we wander, the reason we hide and much more addressed. It addresses the real issues and tragedies of the fall of mankind and how they are lived out in the lives of people today, as it presents biblical and proven solutions. Discussion questions are provided at the end of each chapter.

A Story of Rage
Love's Triumph Over Anger

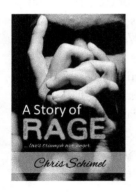

A Story of Rage is a gripping novel that was inspired by actual events. It tells of the life of a young man caught up in a home riddled with the kind of dysfunction that rings way truer and more typical than people in our world would like to admit. You will be shocked and amazed as you watch rage run its course and yet result in redemption you were never able to see coming. This is another of those books you will have difficulty putting down. This presentation is in the form of an E-book.

Ripples
Making Lasting Impact in People's Lives

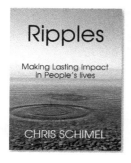

Ripples is mini-book that will help people speak effectively to a mixed crowd of believers and unbelievers in Christ. Too many people wanting to investigate the claims of Christianity and Jesus do not feel comfortable to come to church even one time. They fear they will be made to feel guilty or they won't understand a thing that is said. And most are right. Very few ministers take unbelievers into consideration when they speak. They only address believers because they don't know how to reach unbelievers. Should an unbeliever happen to wander into one of these churches, he or she will often feel as though they don't relate, or worse yet aren't welcome. Ripples teaches how to minister with grace and truth effectively to both.

To acquire any of Chris Schimel's books go to his website. Email him directly for quantity discounts.

To contact Chris...

Website - chrisjschimel.com
email...chrisjschimel@gmail.com